The Challenge for

Evangelical Missions to Europe

Hilkka Mäläskä

The Challenge for
Evangelical

William Carey Library
CHRISTIAN MISSION BOOKS

South Pasadena, California

Missions to Europe

a Scandinavian case study

International Standard Book Number: 0-87808-308-1
Library of Congress Catalog Number: 71-132011

Published by the William Carey Library
533 Hermosa Street
South Pasadena, Calif.   91030
Telephone 213-682-2047

PRINTED IN THE UNITED STATES OF AMERICA

Contents

Part II: What Can Evangelical
Missions Offer?

Appendices

Figures

Foreword

The reader will find much of interest in this thesis by Miss Mäläskä concerning the role of Evangelical Missions in Scandinavia, particularly Finland, her native land.

The historical parts of the thesis show clearly that outside Evangelical interests exercised a profound influence upon church life in Scandinavia, first of all in revitalizing dead churches within the establishment, and then, as the decades went by, in creating fellowships outside the State Churches. So that there is nothing new in an infusion of evangelicalism from abroad. George Scott, for example, was the spiritual grandfather of both the National Evangelical Foundation that operates within the State Church of Sweden, and the Mission Covenant Church that became a Free Church.

It is difficult for the American reader to comprehend a Protestant church establishment. In the United States, people form denominational bodies by mature choices, either by adult decision or by adult confirmation of parental vows. It does not always work like that in a state church establishment. In England, for example, in round figures, 27,000,000 are baptized as infants, 9,000,000 seek confirmation, but only 3,000,000 make their Easter communion, and 1,000,000 are attending church regularly.

There are many deeply spiritual Christians in the State churches of Scandinavia, but many other are those who have regarded their confirmation as graduation---one does not go back to high school after one graduates. So the vital force so often flows in voluntary associations within the State Church or in Free Churches outside it.

Miss Mäläskä reviews the role of the American mission in Scandinavia, its usefulness, its handicaps and even its legitimacy. She writes as a Scandinavian, and says many things that an American would not see or say. And her case concludes on the right note, for in the past the spiritual life of Scandinavia was revitalized by a spiritual awakening, and spiritual revival abroad brought help at critical times.

J. EDWIN ORR, Th.D., D.Phil (Oxon)

Preface

Christianity was first introduced into Scandinavia at the beginning of the ninth century. Soon after the Reformation, Lutheranism was introduced and made Scandinavia the most Lutheran territory in the world. The pure doctrine and formalism was not enough. The Pietists came to direct to a personal faith in Christ. Moravians disturbed the Lutheran conscience with their ardent devotion to the Lamb and with their missionary passion. After the introduction of foreign elements, awakenings occurred in the Scandinavian countries and laymen took the initiative in forming structures for the continuation of Gospel witness. Time after time God raised up new men and sent new awakenings to further His Kingdom on earth.

This is a case study. Examples of different forms and structures are presented from the past and present. These have been evaluated from the church growth point of view, according to the method developed by Dr. Donald A. McGavran. Awakenings, which God sent to refresh His plantation in Scandinavia, later took hold within the State Church or fostered a Free Church. Although this study is more a type of survey—only scratching the surface—its existence is justified as an overall view. Lack of documents in this country has made impossible a thorough, deep study, and records and statistics from abroad have been difficult to obtain by correspondence. In many cases, war has destroyed many important papers. In some cases, the information which was obtained was not useful from the church growth point of view. Libraries have been used in the Los Angeles area and North American mission agencies have rendered helpful assistance, supplying facts concerning their work in Scandinavia.

The writer is of Finnish nationality, formerly connected with the Lutheran State Church of Finland, now a member of the Church of the Nazarene in the United States of America ---thus bringing to this study her personal experience and her observation of church life in Scandinavia.

As a national, the writer has tried to see the case both from the Scandinavian and missionaries' point of view. The motivation for this study has come from the concern over the spiritual laxity in Northern Europe. This also involves the personal struggle of the writer as to whether or not foreign-planted churches are justified in countries where over ninety-five per cent of the population are members of Protestant churches. The writer does not attempt to offer easy solutions. The situation in Scandinavia is too complex to do that. No loyal Scandinavian would humiliate herself voluntarily and admit to the world the spiritual poverty, cold-ness and in some case, the death of churches, if there were not a real need for renewal. No Scandinavian would take the risks involved by suggesting to a foreign mission agency to "come over to Macedonia and help us," if it were not a life and death question. This report assumes that church plant-ing evangelism in Scandinavia is a most urgent necessity. The study has been limited to relevant issues concerning church growth or non-growth, in movements and churches. Concerning Free Churches and movements, special empha-sis has been given to them. The State Church, often unjustly and in unchristian ways, names the other evangelical Pro-testant groups "sects." It has made the already difficult posi-tion of the Free Churches more difficult. The State Church together with the traditional denominations looks upon all newcomers in church planting as "sheep stealers." For the sake of external unity, planting of new churches, which is considered by the World Council of Churches to be sinful, should be avoided! The most touchy questions are---can break away movements, planting new churches and foreign missions in Scandinavia, be justified? Can one be involved in these activities without suffering guilt?

Essentially, this may be called a missions study. It exa-mines the churches and movements in Scandinavia and eval-uates their effectiveness in missionary-minded expansion. It attempts to show the patterns of how the movements and churches have expanded. It analyses the effects of social conditions and mission policies, which have either hindered or stimulated church growth. The purpose of this study is entirely missionary-minded. We have not been concerned so

much with theology as how effective the methods and structures have been for the propagation of the Gospel. It must be
understood that this study is not an attempt to attack any
Church, mission or individual. If criticism occurs, it is
directed towards the structures, methods and ideas.

The historical part of this study is necessary to understand the present and make plans for the future. Especially
in Scandinavia, where traditions are extremely important,
the background of the Churches and movements should not
be ignored. The structures and denominations are only the
outward forms which the Church of Jesus Christ takes here
on earth. These should be flexible so as to meet the real
needs of the people and bring them into obedience to the
Gospel. There is no guarantee that the structures which are
effective in the United States are equally effective in another
culture. Likewise, one should not hold that the structures
of Churches, a hundred years ago, are just as effective today. Showing samples of the various kinds of structural
forms, this study tries to stimulate thinking along this
line---how to most effectively communicate the "faith of
our fathers." Conditions will develop structural patterns in
action.

The Churches grow differently in different countries. Even
among the Scandinavian countries there are distinct differences, each one having a rich heritage, strong national feelings and having varying degrees of response to the Gospel.
After a period of expansion, the Churches usually began to
be interested in institutionalism, thus losing their evangelistic fervor and single mindedness for church planting.
They have lost their passion and vision for evangelism. The
readers will notice this contrast. It should lead the readers
to ask themselves, "What can we learn from the mistakes
of the past?" It should focus attention on the single-minded
pentecostal devotion to Christ and to proclaiming Him crucified and risen, as only Savior and hope of mankind. The short
comings in the past should teach us more persuasive evangelism so as to lead people to Christ, and teach them to be
responsible members of His Church.

In the second part, we discuss the importance of missionary-national communication. Unfortunately this aspect

has been neglected by many mission agencies and mission-aries. Although the difference between the North Americans and Scandinavians does not seem significant at first glance, there are distinct differences and attitudes towards the matters of personal relationship which may cause failure or success on the frontier of missions. From the chapter on missionary-national communication, one should gather how a North American missionary appears to the national, and how some nationals have been tempted to a pattern of life which is an obstruction to church growth and spiritual welfare of the mission. In the following chapters, the present influence of foreign mission agencies is discussed. What kind of an impact have they had? Should new mission agencies be encouraged to come to Scandinavia? If so, what type of missions? Can these be justified? The new church planters will be attacked by the traditional denominations. These chapters reveal some vital facts of declining Churches and low-church minorities. Can a faithful servant of God neglect these receptive people? If the traditional, cold and dormant churches have neglected these people, then there is a case for North American mission agencies. Brief guidelines for church planting are given and realistic suggestions of what type of foreign mission assistance is needed at this hour.

Finally, this study as a whole should be considered as a preliminary to an in-depth study of church growth in the various countries of Scandinavia. There is an urgent need and it should be done for each country separately in the language spoken in each country respectively. The findings should be published and made available to every church leader, pastor, Christian worker and layman in Scandinavia.

This study has been written with the North American audience in mind. Mission agencies, leaders and mission-aries as well as candidates going to Europe as missionaries, could benefit from it. But in all of these needs of challenge and new methods and theory of missions, we should not forget the real key to the problem: a heaven-sent revival. "Not by might, nor by power, but by my spirit, saith the Lord of hosts." (Ezek. 5:6) The visitation of the Holy Spirit as of old, the "mighty rushing wind," will prove to be the dynamic for church growth. He will awaken the sleeping disciples. The lukewarm He makes as a flame of fire. The dead He will give new life.

The writer takes this opportunity of acknowledging indebtedness to Drs. Ralph D. Winter and J. Edwin Orr, who have guided this study, as well as the whole family of the School of World Mission of Fuller Theological Seminary who have been a constant source of inspiration. The writer cannot adequately express her appreciation to all, but thanks the College Church of the Nazarene, Kankakee, Illinois, for their financial contribution towards her education, and the Finnish Lutheran Church of Los Angeles, who provided an electric typewriter for use.

The writer is especially grateful to Mrs. Letty Howe, of Scandinavian descent, who provided her with a scholarship, enabling her to study at the School of World Mission and Institute of Church Growth in Pasadena, California.

The study is offered in the hope that the North American, very patiently, will accommodate his thinking to a different pattern of church life in certain Scandinavian countries, in which members of denominations that are wholly independent bodies in the United States are at the same time members of the official State Churches!

Abbreviations

AEFCOE   American-European Fellowship for Christian Oneness and Evangelization

BCM   Bible Club Movement

BCU   Bible Club Union

CCC   Campus Crusade for Christ

CEF   Child Evangelism Fellowship

EST   Evankelisluterilaisen Sisälähetyssäätion Toimintakertomus

GEM   Greater Europe Mission

IRM   International Review of Missions

MSVKV   Metodistikirkon Suomen Vuosikoneferensin Vuosikirja

N   Navigators

NAPMO   North American Protestant Ministries Overseas Directory

SAYB   Salvation Army Year Book

SGA   Slavic Gospel Association

SELK   Suomen Evankelisluterilainen Kirkko

UPC   United Pentecostal Church

WCH   World Christian Handbook

WLC   World Literature Crusade

YFCI   Youth for Christ International

PART I

Movements for Renewal

1

Movements in the 18th Century

Shortly after 1700, German Pietism entered Scandinavia. King Frederik IV (1699-1730) expressed interest in this new movement by inviting its missionaries to Denmark in 1705 (Hartling, 1964: 56). Frederik IV was not a man with a personal faith in Christ. His wife was German and was well acquainted with the Pietists there, and it is believed that she had much influence over the King, who granted permission to the Pietists to enter Denmark. This new movement was vital and powerful, and good relations were important.

The King assisted the mission efforts of the Pietists by building 240 elementary schools, an orphanage in Copenhagen and a printing press (Hartling 1964: 56-57). This press was the most important, for it supplied devotional literature to all of Scandinavia. Church attendance became compulsory in Denmark. Confirmation was introduced in 1736, including pre-Bible study and the Catechism. The Pietists also made a strong impact upon Scandinavia through their hymns, and emphasized the priesthood of all believers. The Church, they held, existed not only for theologians and ministers. It consisted not only of doctrine, but of practice. Pietism was severe on the clergy, disturbing their false contentment in resting upon theological education rather than piety. Pietism confronted ministers with the Gospel, and expected them to preach so that common people could obtain spiritual help.

The ideals of Pietism were 1) the salvation of the individual; and 2) the ecclesiola in ecclesia, a church within a church. The Kingdom of God was to be separated from the State, from its political and financial interests. Pietism introduced "free enterprise" in the Church, setting missions apart from State direction.

The Moravians

King Christian VI (1730-1746), son of King Frederik IV, had already adopted Pietism while a pupil in a pietist school. As a believer in Christ, King Christian VI had friendly relations with Count Zinzendorf. The King had a tendency towards separatism. Zinzendorf visited him first in the early 1730s to consider the possibilities for Moravian work in the country. After his accession to the throne, Christian VI rather adopted churchly Pietism. This resulted in more restrictions upon free gatherings to worship. The parish priest had to be informed of all meetings which were to take place outside the State Church. It was unfortunate that the Pietists had accepted any kind of assistance and help from the government. Their sincere plans first to win the important people ended up with the State becoming an intolerable straight-jacket upon the Church.

Count Zinzendorf

The Bible says that not many noble are called, but Count Zinzendorf was among the few. Of his countrymen, he was the only one among the noblemen to take a clear stand for Christ. From his earliest boyhood, he was known to have good habits. Thompson gives this account:

When the army of Charles XII of Sweden was in Saxony, a party of soldiers intruding themselves into the Castle of Hennersdorf, and into the room where the Count, only six years old, was at prayer, were so impressed by the earnestness of his devotions that they paused in silence, and soon withdrew. (Thompson, 1882: 43-44)

Zinzendorf seemed to be lifted above earthly things. Worldly gain did not interest him. He was sincere in his devotion to Christ.

At the age of nineteen, at the wish of his parents, Count Zinzendorf set out on a tour of the continent. On this trip this young nobleman met several representatives from different faiths. This helped convince him more and more that religion of the heart was the correct one. When he came to the Art Gallery at Dusseldorf, he saw Dominico Feti's great painting, Ecce Homo, a picture of the crucified Christ. The words, "All this I did for thee; what doest thou for me?" challenged him. It was here he received his call to be a missionary.

The deep dedication which possessed Zinzendorf made him a flame of fire among cold nominal Christians. Even his marriage was influenced by his commitment. Concerning his fiancee, he wrote to the Countess:

She will have to cast all ideas of rank and quality to the winds, as I have done; for they are not things of divine institution, but inventions of human vanity. If she wishes to aid me she must give herself to what is the sole object of my life; namely, to win souls to Christ and that in the midst of contemporary reproach   (Thompson, 1882 : 70).

Zinzendorf set up strict rules for missionaries, but he was also the first one to be an example in keeping them. The modern missionary agencies have suffered much because of lack of discipline. Winter points out:

We don't have the personal discipline that we ought to have. The average missionary could double his effec – tiveness if he were in a harness of greater supervision. Missionaries suffer from the lack of this. They need tighter discipline, many of them (Winter, 1969 : 305).

Zinzendorf challenged his missionaries to be content, and seek nothing for themselves, not honor, nor mention of fame. They had to be ready to die and to be forgotten. They had to trust the Lord one hundred percent for their future in all matters. There were no alternatives for discipline: "If you take a penny more than you need," Zinzendorf told George Schmidt, "I will dismiss you from the service " (Lewis, 1968 : 92). However, Zinzendorf never lacked for volunteer missionaries.

The promptness and obedience of the Moravian missionaries was habitual. Many of the missionaries were given only twenty four hour notice before being sent to the field. When Ladyard, upon his return to England, was asked by Zinzendorf if he was willing to set out again, he answered promptly: "Tomorrow morning." Sir Colin Campbell went to India after twenty-four hours notice. Another Moravian was sent to the field after Zinzendorf asked this question:

"Will you go to Greenland tomorrow as a missionary?" His reply was: "If the shoemaker can finish the boots that I have ordered of him by tomorrow, I will go." (Thompson, 1882: 470)

Zinzendorf had a dream, a plan to witness in terms of the whole world. "I have but one passion, and it is He, He only," Zinzendorf said. But without his soldiers, he would have been helpless. He had the talent to organize them into societies, giving them a fitting standard. "I admit no Christianity without Fellowship," he declared.

The Lamb to whom Zinzendorf had pledged his devotion and loyalty shaped his personality so as to be most useful. He was at ease among all people.

He asked no special favours or circumstances for himself. He was a rich noble, but he made long itineraries on foot, travelling incognito and living on such food as kindly disposed folks offered him. He had no press agents and he did not organize tent or tabernacle meetings. He regarded mass meetings for evangelism as mobs or grand spectacles rather than agencies of the Lamb. He spoke to anybody, to peasants and nobles, to gypsies, to beggars, to travellers on foot, on horse-back, in coach-and-four; he held devotional meetings in cottages and castles, in universities and hostels; and singing-services for himself and any of his company as they made their way through the land. He picked up orphans and helpless old people and arranged for them to be sent and to be cared for in Herrnhut. (Lewis, 1962: 122-123).

There is no doubt that Zinzendorf's outstanding devotion and commitment contributed largely to the success he had in his missionary work.

Thompson testifies:

If all Protestant churches had been equally devoted, equally enterprising, for the last century and a half, not one unevangelized man or woman would now remain on earth (Thompson, 1882 : 488).

Not only was Zinzendorf a poet, hymn-writer, teacher, administrator, ecclesiastical statesman, but he was also a missionary in the fullest sense of the word.

Missionary Methods

Special attention should be given Zinzendorf's care for his members. When a new denomination was in its first stage, there were meetings almost every day. A new born baby needs more nurture than does an adult. Zinzendorf saw this need of a qualitative church growth emphasizing holiness of life.

He also planned a method of visitation whereby every member was approached at least every fourteen days. The visitors would converse with the members during walks or in the house, before or after working hours. Sometimes a visitor would suddenly step into a workshop and, without saying a word, look at his brethren. The look was well understood; it conveyed the inquiry, Is the Lamb in your thoughts? (Lewis, 1962: 65).

In the Moravian community there were at least three meetings a day for the whole congregation. They were conducted with reverence. The members were aware that they were in the presence of the Lamb. The day in the Moravian communities began with singing in the assembly hall as is usually done in many European Bible Schools. During the winter the day started at five o'clock and during the summer at four. Every age level of the family was recognized. Special services for children, the infirmed, and the aged were conducted.

The chief objective of the Moravian community was to be obedient to the Great Commission. Herrnhut became the center for the world enterprise. Their missionaries kept in mind two principles: their members ought to organize themselves like communities, and they were to win souls.

The Mission to Scandinavia

Zinzendorf visited Copenhagen to attend the coronation of King Christian VI, because of personal friendship. Count Zinzendorf also had a plan at the same time to start a Moravian Community in Denmark. It was four years later, in 1735, that he dispatched two Danes, Piper and Gert Hansen, to Denmark to find out what possibilities there were for

Moravian work. They found there a small group of Danish pastors who had been converted through the influence of Pietism. They were greatly moved by the preaching of the two Moravians and later became instruments for revival. The island, Fyn, represents the oldest area for Moravian missions in Scandinavia. By 1740 the Moravians had about 200 members there. In 1770 the number declined to 75, but it increased again in 1800 to about 300 members. It is believed that this change was due to financial circumstances in the community (Thyssen 1967, Vol. 4, 29ff)

Moravian work began in Christiansfeld in 1727 (Thyssen, Vol. 4:29). This community was founded as a result of the missionary efforts of the immigrants and the revival. The King of Denmark was favorable towards the efforts of the Moravians and in gratitude to the King, this community was named after him. The community was set up as a city of brotherhood and a corresponding agency set up to meet each need. These agencies operated through councils. The most important one was the Elder Council, consisting of two members. The Inspector Council, composed of a few select members from the community, was responsible for inspecting the morals, etc. of members. The Great Helper Conference had to give guidance and examine important affairs whenever this was needed by the Congregation Council. This Council was concerned with practical matters. The village style was typically German, quite similar to the community in Herrnhut which had an old city plan of parallel streets (Thyssen, 1967, Vol. 4 : 40).

Regulations

There was no private life in the community. The opposite sexes could only meet when absolutely necessary. All talk of marriage was forbidden. Those who were already married agreed to raise up their children strictly after the Christian standards set up by the community. The children were also separated according to their sex. All visitors were to be reported to the leader of the community. Borrowing money was held a sin (Thyssen 1967, Vol. 4: 51-52). Brotherliness was practised in the fellowship and the rules were never burden some to those who lived in this puritanical society.

Attitude toward the State Church

The Moravians strictly preached true conversion and the difference between believers and non-believers was clearly recognized. They were never ashamed of their intention, of trying to convert all the people in Denmark (Thyssen, 4: 174). The Moravians were well aware of the importance of their mission. They did not openly criticise the State Church ministers. However, it was noticeable in other ways, they talked about the "real" ministers, those who had a personal faith in Christ. The others were not worth mentioning.

The Influence of the Moravians

The purpose of the Danish Moravianism was to plant a church for their Savior in Denmark (Thyssen, Vol. 4: 106). The Moravians did missionary trips from the community to other areas of the country establishing diaspora work. From the beginning the community consisted mostly of Danes, although some foreigners came in from Germany as well as from Sweden and Norway (Thyssen 1967: 4 95).

Moravianism came to Sweden also through a national as was the case in Denmark. In 1735, Zinzendorf visited Sweden personally and found some church leaders friendly towards them. In spite of opposition from the State Church, about three per cent of their ministers favored the Moravians and their beliefs (Latourette, 1958 : 86).

The Moravian missionaries went also to Lapland in 1734 for a couple of years. When they saw that the people there were under the care of the Lutheran State Church, they returned (Thompson, 1882 : 458). Moravians were known to stay clear from the other churches to keep friendly relations (Lewis, 1962 : 131).

The present Moravian Church in Denmark has stopped growing and numbers about 300 members. Moravians have likewise stopped growing in other Scandinavian countries--- indeed, this appears to be the universal pattern. They have been like leaven in their service to other churches. The Methodist Church is greatly indebted to the Moravians. The Moravians pointed the way to assurance of salvation to Wesley. Indirectly, the Moravians influenced millions in becoming Christians through Wesley.

Why has Moravian growth been so small? As a Protestant monasticism, the community functioned as a refuge for Christians under persecution. It became an ideal community copied from the first Christians, and it had an outstanding spiritual quality.

However, community living gives one the impression of weak Christians who can not tolerate any opposition in the world. On the other hand, this kind of living-in situation is of great importance to newly born believers. When we understand the background of Denmark, the Viking period with its immorality and broken homes, we can understand more fully why this kind of community was necessary in Denmark to encourage the new converts.

The Moravian community operated a twenty-four hourly-program, taking care of the complete person. Its members did not share their material belongings, but instead each of them had the right to keep his own possessions; otherwise, the community was all-embracing.

It is always much easier to build a church than to build a city. About the year 1800, the Moravian community developed financial difficulties. This also caused the membership to drop considerably (Thyssen, 4:40). The Moravians' non-aggressive attitude towards evangelism was probably yet an added reason for hindering their church growth, as was the lack of capable leadership after Zinzendorf's death.

The life of the eighteenth century Moravians was not an easy one. Lewis's account of Zinzendorf and his followers seems true in its judgments:

> The Pietists resented his success; the Lutherans regarded him as a separatist; the nobility (including his mother and aunt Henrietta) felt that he had disgraced their rank   (Lewis, 1962 : 122).

In some ways, the Moravian movement was a success; in others, it failed. They were the great champions of "heart-religion" in the eighteenth century, and they possessed 'the greatest of all visions' of their time, that of 'discipling' the nations of the earth. This task was passed on to nineteenth century missions.

Figure 1

THE SPREAD OF THE FINNISH EVANGELICAL LUTHERAN REVIVAL
MOVEMENTS IN 1960s

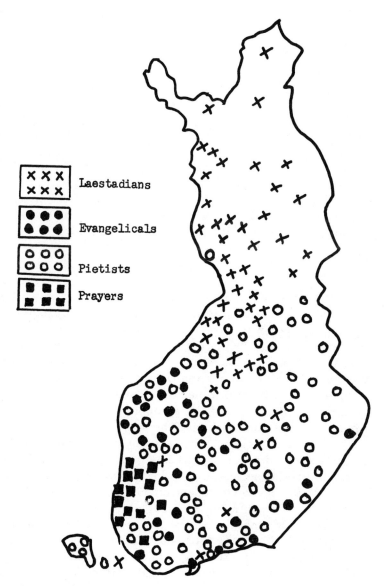

Source: Haavio 1968:39,52,69,81.

Movements in the 19th Century

Finland

In the nineteenth century, the nobility and clergy in Finland supported the objectives of the German Enlightenment, which were not against Christianity as such, but were aimed at "enlightening" the Church. This widened the gap between the clergy and the common people. The masses felt that they were not receiving the necessary spiritual food in the church. In their spiritual hunger they turned to the old pietist literature, hoping to find solutions to their spiritual problems. Some even turned to an old heathen magic, which was quite strong, especially in the isolated communities.

The Pietists

The Pietist Movement is the best known of the four Awakening Movements in Finland. It began quite spontaneously among the people themselves. Its beginning has been traced to the year 1796 when some workers on a Savolax farm enjoyed an ecstatic experience, which spread to neighboring communities; and among many others, Paavo Ruotsalainen, a farmer from Nilsia, joined the movement. His personality and spirituality became the symbol of Finnish Pietism, for (though simple and unlearned) he was sought by thousands.

In his early years, Ruotsalainen had obtained a Bible, a very rare and precious gift in those days. He had read it through three times before the age of sixteen. As he was unable to write, he had to depend on friends to write his letters later on to those in need who sought his help.

Although Ruotsalainen lived in a religious environment, he was unable to find peace in his soul for such a long period of time. This inner conflict constantly upset him. His family and friends were concerned, afraid that he would lose his mind. But Ruotsalainen heard about a blacksmith, Jaakko

Hogman, who was firmly grounded in the faith. Hogman, being already acquainted with the Moravian missions in northern Finland, gave Ruotsalainen this advice: "You lack one thing. You have not experienced Christ within yourself." This statement was well taken and the experience of Christ within became a reality. After this experience he became the great spiritual leader of Finland, having the privilege also of guiding both laymen and clergy in matters spiritual. As a central figure in the Awakening movement, Ruotsalainen had one primary aim---to lead seekers to Christ.

"Paavo," as Paavo Ruotsalainen was known to the Finnish people, preached that the way of the Lord was the way of the Cross. This way leads to humility not greatness. We are not holy but sinners who need daily repentance. In one sense, it was a "beggar" religion, for people were admonished to long constantly for and wait upon the Lord. If one came to believe that he knew that he was saved, he was thought to have already fallen from his faith. God resists the proud. Ruotsalainen feared so much the false security and "brain religion" in the State Church that he went to the other extreme. Spiritual poverty became the characteristic of Finnish Pietism. People had to long and wait for the Lord constantly. There was no assurance of salvation, such as Evangelicals experience. So both good and bad in Finnish Christianity were seen in Ruotsalainen.

The missionary methods of the Pietists took the form of "seurat"---or "gatherings". These gatherings took place in private homes. The origin of this is typically Finnish. The gatherings were informal, where everyone who wished had the opportunity to speak. The numbers of the hymns sung were never announced. Usually one began to sing and then others joined in. The speakers spoke freely from the heart without any preparation. Each person started his talk with a testimony, and there could be several speakers at one meeting. Each speaker followed the thoughts of the one ahead, and so the meeting resulted in a real continuity of thought. After they had sung an old Moravian-style hymn in mournful tones, an after-meeting followed, in which there was first, confession, then forgiveness, a time for pastoral care.

The Pietists wore their own uniform, and their dress dated back to the eighteenth century, a mode that was then used by the nobility. The men's outfits were grey and the women's were blue with a black scarf. Their hairstyle also made them appear separate from the world, worn with their hair always parted in the middle.

Their strict rules governing behavior forbade their own young people having fellowship with people who were outside their group. On the other hand, the Pietists had a strong unity among themselves. They were always eager to help their fellow believers in various ways when the need arose, and this promoted good morale.

The Pietists were not without a sense of humor that often showed in private conversation. This was understandable, for their life in the lonely farm-houses in the forests held many hardships caused by man and nature. The melancholy mood of their religious life, caused by these hardships, in turn affected their attitudes. They were truly, as they said themselves, "miserable saints."

In the first part of the nineteenth century, the movement met strong opposition caused by government officials and by church leaders, concerned about this mass movement among the people and afraid of a revolution against Russian rule.

The Pietists, or "Coat-tailers" (korttilainen), as other Finns nicknamed them because of their coat tails having three slits, nevertheless grew rapidly in numbers. Notably they attracted several hundred State Church priests; and as many as 20,000 people from all over the country gathered for their annual summer meetings out in the open. Through the first half of the century, they continued (Sentze, 1963:81).

The growth and success of the Pietist movement reached its peak in the 1840s. The people were still first generation Pietists. But then the second and the following generations, as in any religious organization, brought the kiss of death to the movement. The children of the pioneers killed the vitality of the movement by their formality.

In the 1840s, splits began among the Pietists. Following these, their religious life was very passive till 1880 when a refreshing renewal took place under the leadership of Wilhelm Malmivaara.

Figure 1 shows the areas to which the Pietist movement
spread since the early 19th century. The Pietists now main-
tain People's High Schools where their children are educated
in the faith of their fathers. Present Pietist strength is estimated at more than 13,800, the number of subscriptions to
their official periodical, possibly 40,000 as a constituency
(Kuoppala 1970).

The Praying Movement

The movement referred to as the "Praying Ones" is the
oldest as well as the smallest of the four Finnish Awakening
movements. This old organization dates back to the great
religious awakening toward the end of the eighteenth century
when the Spirit of God swept over the nation. It received its
inspiration from the radical pietism of the eighteenth century
as well. In the beginning, it was a common occurrence for
people to experience an ecstasy, but later this disappeared
at the beginning of the nineteenth century (Haavio, 1965:30).
Henrik Renqvist, the leader of the Praying Ones, was
influenced by various groups, especially by the Moravians.
Kneeling in prayer was of great importance. As in the early
Pietism, several special requirements for salvation were
stressed; repentance, faith and a new life. If only one of
these steps was bypassed, then their whole Christian experience collapsed. They also stressed the Second Coming
of Christ more than the other Finnish revival movements.
Henrik Renqvist had been acquainted with the Pietists
and Paavo Ruotsalainen and his community. This did not
result in a clear understanding in his own religious life. Dis-
appointed, he dropped out of school where he was studying to
be a priest in the State Church. He then began to sell devotional material instead. However, because of encouragement from his friends, Renqvist resumed his studies again
and thereafter grew in his spiritual life.
After his ordination, he met with much indifference among
the "Christian Finns." The people spent their Sabbath days
drinking, and it was not unusual for them to attend Church
while under the influence of liquor. Only about twenty percent of the adults were able to read, which was one reason

for the poor knowledge of Christianity. There were people in the community who even practised witchcraft as a profession (Juva, 1966: 237-238).

In his preaching, Renqvist described in plain language the fires of Hell. He dismissed the old inspectors of the community and trained new officials required to forward him a report of all prostitutes, drinkers, witches and those who sought their help, those who played cards, blasphemers, quarrelsome persons, and the like, for action (Juva, 1966: 238). This resulted in his parishoners living a better life. He was strict, and wished the Christians to show signs of holiness in their everyday living. Prayer was of great importance, but he could not stand any ecstatic experience. When someone tried to speak in tongues, he was immediately carried out of the meeting (Juva, 1966: 238).

The movement still follows the old devotional literature and the old Bible translation. They will not part from these old books. The fear that a worldly spirit would influence their thinking through reading modern books has made the Praying Movement ineffective in present day society. The old language does not speak to today's youth. In some churches where the movement still is strong, even the worship services are conducted from the old church manual and hymns from the hymnbook of 1701 are still sung (Haavio, 1965: 31).

"The Praying Ones" also gathered in private homes, where all knelt when praying. Hymns were sung and spontaneous talks were given. Hymns could be interrupted when someone said: "Let us pray for grace now." Everyone then took turns in prayer, from little children to bishops and government officials.

The movement acknowledged the authority of the State Church. They were not an aggressive type of people. They firmly believed that as long as the "Our Father" was read in the State Church, they must not leave it (Haavio, 1965: 32). "But one circumstance complicated the extension of their faith. They have no leader and few descendants" (Sentzke, 1963: 90). The present estimate of the supporters of the Praying Movement is about 2,700. Figure number 1 shows the spread of the movement. It has ceased to grow in Southwest Finland.

The Evangelical Movement

The Evangelical movement is a split from the Pietist Movement. In 1840, the first crisis began when Frederik Gabriel Hedberg, the founder of the new movement, recognized that the Pietists did not have much assurance of salvation. The Pietists were too concerned with their sin. They were continually longing for the light. Hedberg believed that God wished His children to rejoice about their salvation.

Hedberg was converted when he was a lad of fourteen. It was while studying for the ministry later, that he had a crisis in his life while reading some of the Pietist and Moravian literature. He felt that there was a conflict between the two and it was not until after he had read Luther's works that he felt enlightened concerning religious questions. Hedberg's theological emphasis was the assurance of salvation, and God's promises in His Word and also in infant baptism. This emphasis later resulted in the schism from the Pietists in 1844, but it was well received by the clergy and many who joined him.

In all of the Finnish revival movements, it was not uncommon for the followers of the leaders to misunderstand the significance of their special emphasis, which soon became a requirement for becoming a Christian. The history of these movements reveal a picture of disharmony among the people. (Finland has yet to see two religious bodies getting along with one another.) The differences between the Pietists and Evangelicals was so small, yet they felt it necessary to part. The Evangelicals expressed their joy spontaneously in worldly songs and dances (Juva, 1966: 254); but Finnish Christians had never bothered to study the facts for themselves, instead preferring to believe the rumors saying that Hedberg and all his supporters had backslidden and gone back into the world. The Pietists as well as the Evangelicals listened to these rumors as well, and the gap between Hedberg and Ruotsalainen was widened considerably. They never tried to get together to come to any agreement between themselves.

The Evangelicals held their meetings in private homes, for careful Bible Study. Usually, they attended a Lutheran church where there was an evangelical pastor.

As this movement attracted many gifted ministers, it succeeded in the literary mission of translating Luther's writings into the Finnish language. The lay missionaries distributed these as well as other devotional material among the people.

Special Gospel Festivals were arranged in the nineteenth century that later became a tradition in the organization. The purpose of these Festivals was to create fellowship among the members and to train them in doctrine. The gatherings drew as many as 10,000 people. They came from great distances in spite of primitive transportation and communication conditions. However, these Gospel Festivals proved to be a great inspiration to the members.

During the period of 1870-90, the Evangelical movement reached its peak in growth. It attracted more people in the West where people were more open-minded and affected by Swedish influences. There were several Evangelical communities in Southern Finland up to the border of Savolax. Figure number 1 shows how the Evangelical groups spread.

Haavio points out three periods in the history of the Evangelicals. First, the period of rapid growth, 1870-1890; second, the period after 1895 when the work was officially recognized by the Church; third, the period which began around 1930, when formalism took over this movement (Haavio, 1965: 60-63).

The statistics of the year 1963 show the membership of the Evangelicals to be 19,893. They employed five ministers and about forty full-time laymen. The organization has 102 meeting-halls   (Haavio, 1965: 64).

The Evangelical movement has had its own mission work in Japan since 1898. Their influence on the home land has been the protection of Luther's writings as well as making them known to their people.

The Laestadians

The Laestadian movement derived its name from Lars Levi Laestadius, its founder. It originated in Swedish Lappland where by 1840 its spiritual impact was already being felt. From Sweden, this revival spread rapidly to Finland

and Norway as well as to other parts of Sweden. It tended to succeed in those areas where the Finnish language was spoken. This fourth movement in Northern Finland had different historical roots to the other three, yet it does not appear that it was less meaningful than the others.

Laestadius was a son of a minister in Swedish Lappland. His father gave in to his strong temptation for alcohol so his was a poor home. Laestadius began to study for the ministry, realizing that he did not have a true religious experience. He made the same observation of his parishioners.

The beginnings of the Laestadian movement took place at a very dark and discouraging time. Drunkenness, immorality and broken homes were common. In the nineteenth century, the church in Lappland was mostly a mission effort although Lappland was formally Christianized in the seventeenth century. As a background to the Laestadian movement, we need to take note of the mission work of the Pietists and Moravians. Their missionary efforts were carried on by voluntary laymen during the eighteenth century. In Sweden, the "Läsare" or "Readers" contributed to the Laestadians, especially in the north. The "Readers" had been influenced by the Pietists and Moravians. Both Luther's writings, and pietist literature sowed the seed of the Gospel.

Theologically their heritage was Pietistic and partly Moravian. Pietism put the emphasis on repentance and a contrite heart and 'liikutukset,' "emotions," as a sign of grace. The Moravians contributed their emphasis on blood mysticism, emotions and comfort from the Word for those who repented. Sermons of Laestadian missionaries were open and sincere messages of the terribleness of sin and hell. Bergroth hated the crudeness of the language in the sermons of the Laestadian missionaries. However, it should be understood that the level of the people to whom they ministered was not high intellectually. Their manner of living was such that this vulgar language did not offend them. The messages were well received and were well understood (Bergroth, 1902: 853). Many of the Lapps still clung to their pagan beliefs and alcohol wrought great havoc. This caused and inspired Laestadius to preach the moral law even more, until his own conversion through the testimony of a Lapp girl.

The Laestadian movement held a critical and negative attitude towards the world and especially towards other Christians. They believed strongly that their kind of Christianity was the only true kind. Vulgar and offensive terms are still used by them.

In 1854, Laestadius' coworker, J. Raatamaa, introduced confession into the movement. He noticed it in Luther's works, and it proved to be an effective means in winning converts.

Private confession takes place in all of the Laestadian groups. Sometimes the confession has to be made before the congregation. The church invites confession for forgiveness. The normal procedure now is for a person to confess to a Christian whom he chooses and can trust. Then a confession to the church follows, this being a formal one. Knowing the very reserved nature of the Finns in northern Finland, this is by no means an easy procedure. Those who have complied with this procedure feel that they are the only true kind of Christian. The Laestadian group believe that they hold the Keys to the Kingdom. There are moments of great tension before confession, but followed by outbursts of joy and ecstacy.

The Laestadians are not warm towards the Church, even though they belong to it and let their children be baptized, and celebrate their Communion in the State Church. When they speak of their spiritual home, they mean the Laestadian movement and its local gatherings.

The Laestadians still believe that it is a sin to wear a tie or a watch, to use or own a bicycle, car, radio or a television set. A good Laestadian will not use any curtains in his home either.

Due to the narrowminded, sectarian spirit of the Laestadians, they have split into three groups: the first-born, the newly awakened, and the conservatives. The first-born group are legalistic and ascetic. Its sectarian teaching holds firmly that one denomination can be God's representative on earth---the first-born. This privilege was passed on directly from the primitive church to them. This group spread mostly during 1920-40 in the southern and central cities of Finland. After they set up seventeen congregations, the church grew no more (Haavio, 1965: 77).

The Newly-Awakened were organized in 1896 and missionaries began their work immediately. Their work spread along the rivers in some communities in Lappland and in the West. This group was especially missionary minded. In 1907, their own missionary society was formed.

The Conservative group was the main branch of the Laestadians and also the largest from which the First-Born and the Newly-Awakened separated. The reasons for these splits were minor ones. They consisted of the different values laid on confession and morality.

Figure number 1 shows the spread of the Laestadians in Finland. The southern border line has not altered since 1870. They have not had success in the South. The isolated environment in which the people live in the North may have contributed somewhat, in that the movement has appealed only to certain types of people living in certain areas.

The Laestadian movement has lacked good organization and as a result their growth has been small. Also the enforced confession and conservative way of life have been barriers too great to overcome. Their missionary approach was very crude. There was cursing and fighting that sometimes led to someone being knocked out if he failed to embrace the Laestadian faith. Their missionaries succeeded in influencing the people to be temperate.

The Lutheran Church in Finland should not have been so critical of the Free Churches there with their informal type of worship. They should have studied awakening movements in their own church more closely. The ecstasy of the Laestadians with their overflowing emotions was an example. It is easier to see the "mote that is in thy brother's eye," but not to consider "the beam that is in thine own eye." (Matt. 7:3) These four Finnish awakening movements in the nineteenth century were as a fresh breeze in the State Church, which stirred the laymen even though this resulted in their introducing their own favorite ideas of the Word of God. They did contribute much to Christian morals, temperance and patriotism. It should be noted, however, that the Communist party in Finland won the highest number of votes in the areas where the Laestadians were the strongest (Haavio, 1965: 74).

Norway

Hans Nielsen Hauge

Nineteenth century Norway enjoyed many refreshing times of awakening, wave after wave of spiritual revival.

Christianity had been attacked in several ways. A militant secularism had gained strength, but the seed sown in the eighteenth century was not in vain. The ground was prepared for the lay awakenings within the Church of Norway.

Hans Nielsen Hauge (1771-1824) was born into a simple farm family in Norway. He showed great interest in reading early in life, more especially in devotional literature that was available in his time. Through a State church priest, Gerhard Seeberg, who came and brought his library with him to Tune in 1778, Hauge was more and more stimulated in his Christian experience.

At the age of sixteen, Hauge was confirmed, following the custom in the State Church. This act made a strong impact upon his life. A sudden transformation took place. The opposition from the world was so strong that he was forced to leave his home village for a while (Aarflot, 1967: 236).

At the invitation of his parents, he came back home to work in the fields on April 5, 1796, when he experienced a new confrontation with God. While at work one spring day, Hauge sang his favorite hymn: "Jesus, I long for the blessed communion," and then proceeded to the next verse:

> Mightily strengthen my spirit within me,
> That I may learn what Thy Spirit can do.
> O take Thou captive each passion within me,
> Lead me and guide me my whole journey through.
> All that I am and possess I surrender,
> If Thou alone in my spirit mayst dwell,
> All will I yield Thee, my Saviour, most tender,
> Take me and own me, and all will be well.

Pettersen calls this Hauge's "Pentecostal baptism" (Pettersen, 1921: 53). Molland says that it reminds one of Wesley's experience at the Aldersgate Street prayer meeting, 1738--- when his heart was 'strangely warmed.' And Hauge himself testified:

Something supernatural filled my soul. It was divine
and wonderful. Words cannot describe it. I remember
it as if it were today, although it is twenty years ago.
God's love overflowed me. No one can take it from
me, of this I am confident. This is the inner burning
love to God and people. My soul was transformed after
I repented of all my sins. I long for people to share
this same grace with me. I received a special love of
reading the Holy Scripture to learn what Jesus thought.
I received light to understand it. All Christ's teachings pointed out that He came here to be our Saviour.
Through His Spirit we are born again and are sancti-
fied to be more like Him; to serve the Triune God and
prepare our souls for everlasting happiness. It was
then when I saw the world fallen into deep sin. It
caused me much pain to look at it. I asked God to de-
lay His judgement so that some would have an opportunity to be saved. Now I was willing to serve God and
I prayed that He would reveal to me what I should do.
The voice said in my soul: "You shall confess my
Name to all people; encourage them to be saved and
seek Me while they can find Me; call upon Me when I
am present and touch their hearts, then will they come
from darkness to light   (Aarflot, 1967:237-8)

This testimony which Hauge wrote in 1815 describes the
spirit and ministry of this lay preacher very well. Hauge's
life after this Pentecostal experience can be divided into
three periods: His missionary travels from 1796 to 1804;
imprisonment from 1804 to 1814, and the period of quiet-
ness when he worked on the farm again and at the same time
took over the leadership of the Norway-wide awakening, till
his death   (Aarflot, 1967: 241).

After his call to service, Hauge traveled widely in Norway preaching wherever he had the opportunity. In some
places he found small Christian groups which had come from
Pietist and Moravian awakenings. He made most of his trips
on foot. Where people took him into their house, Hauge went
to work with the farmers in the fields. He always identified
himself with the farmers, who had been suppressed and forgotten by others   (Molland, 1963: 15).

Hauge was in prison for the second period of his ministry, In 1804, a Lutheran bishop accused him of having too strong an influence in the diocese and it seemed that he could be politically dangerous (Aarflot, 1967: 245). Hauge was condemned to prison for violating the conventicle law of 1741.

The latter part of his life, Hauge devoted to writing. He wrote over forty different pieces of literature, which he bound himself to reduce the cost of publication. All this literature was distributed at no cost. Through this method of evangelism, a generation of Norwegians came in contact with the spirit and message of Hauge.

Hauge was said to be the greatest preacher in Norway. He was a typical Norwegian and he brought a national spirit to the country (Pettersen, 1921: 34). We say that England is a different place because John Wesley lived. In the same sense we could say that Norway is different because of Hauge.

Haugeanism

The Haugean Awakening, with its emphasis on conversion and holiness, has sometimes been referred to as a puritan movement in Norway. Warm devotion and contentment were characteristic of the Haugeans. This movement never became an independent free church. It was rather a church within a Church. Hauge and his adherents always wanted to be connected with the Lutheran Church, and Hauge set an example for them by faithfully attending the services of the Lutheran Church. The Haugean meetings were never held in opposition to the State Church services.

The inner structure of the Haugean movement is not easy to describe. First of all, it is a fellowship of believers in Christ, bound together spiritually by the Holy Spirit. Having a good attitude towards the State Church, the Haugeans lifted the nation socially by encouraging its adherents to be active in politics as well as in social matters.

Hauge encouraged church growth internally by introducing a lay movement. He concentrated on the farmers who were receptive to the Gospel, and in the cities he sought to win those who came from rural areas. The Haugeans practised the priesthood of believers. The lay-workers carried on the work while Hauge was in prison and the movement reached its peak in 1824. By 1840 it was difficult to see any difference between the Haugeans and other groups. (Latourette, 1959:156) The Haugeans became a model for other lay movements and organizations to follow.

The Norwegian Lutheran Inner Mission Society (Det Norske Lutherske Indremisjonsselskap)

The political situation in Norway had become democratic and as a result lay preachers were more readily accepted among the people. In 1888, lay preaching in State Churches was legally permitted, although lay preachers were not allowed to preach from the pulpit.

The Norwegian Lutheran Inner Mission Society reached its present stage through a long process of development. It was influenced by the Haugean movement, the Johnson awakening, which was later known as the Luther Foundation (Lutherstiftelsen). This was reorganized in 1891, and now bears the name, The Norwegian Lutheran Inner Mission Society. Norwegians call it Indremisjon.

The Johnson Awakening

In 1850-60 a new awakening swept across the country. It was so called because the leading personality in the movement was that of Professor Gisle Johnson. It was surprising that this learned man was able to communicate and reach the common people so well. He spoke in very simple language and was therefore clearly understood. It is also true that an epidemic spread throughout the country at the same time (1853), and the capital city was especially hard hit. These trials caused the resistance of the people to be very low, but they were still very receptive to the preaching of the Gospel.

Johnson turned over responsibility of preaching to laymen, who were able to continue the work when he was set aside. This awakening reached all social classes all over the country. The reason for this, said Molland, was that there were ministers of the Lutheran Church in charge

(Molland, 1968: 35). The presence of the State Church ministers in the movement caused people to change their suspicious attitudes towards the awakenings. Johnson himself was a committed Lutheran, and wished to keep the doctrine unadulterated. The name "Lutheran" was applied to all that was begun by Johnson and his disciples. Because of this label, the movement was readily accepted everywhere (Molland, 1968: 37).

Johnson and his adherents did not have the same standard of spirituality as did the Haugeans. They did not have the puritanical ideas of the Pietists either, for Johnson himself was a smoker and he allowed young people to dance in his house (Molland, 1968: 37). However, the outside world only knew him as a serious preacher who pleaded for people to accept Christ.

The ministers in the Johnson awakening were the spokesmen for Evangelical Christianity. The State Church was their missionfield, and they were the missionaries. They were proud to be evangelists. Personal faith in Jesus Christ was of great importance and emphasis was given to the conditions for eligibility to take communion. Only believers had the right to take communion (1968: 38). The ministers advocated that confession was to take place in the presence of a minister before taking communion.

The believers of the Johnson awakening organized themselves into small groups in differnt parts of the country wherever they happened to be located. In many places, the laymen called a State Church minister to be their leader. In this way they were able to use the State Church property for their meetings. However, there continued to be tensions because of the Inner Mission's attitude towards the Sacraments and communion in the State Church. This finally resulted in the founding of the Luther Foundation in 1868.

The Luther Foundation (Lutherstiftelsen)

Gisle Johnson was one of the men who founded the Luther Foundation. The idea for this came from Sweden where the Evangelical Mission Society (Evangeliska Fosterlandstiftelsen) had been started. This was a central organization composed of all the small inner missions in Sweden. From Norway, Johnson observed the development of the Swedish Evangelical Mission Society over a period of ten years, writing regular reports for the Inner Mission magazines.

After the Luther Stiftelsen was finally organized in 1868, it resulted in much church growth. About thirty groups in the nation joined the organization in the first year. In 1870 some reorganization took place again resulting in fifty groups. All church groups were permitted to join this organization (Aarflot, 1967:386). In 1877 the Luther Foundation sponsored eighty one laymen preaching all over the country.

The annual meetings were of great importance to the evangelical people of Norway. They were a minority in the country and they were encouraged by attending a large gathering of believers. Attendance at these annual meetings was sometimes over ten thousand (1967: 390).

The success of the small groups in the State Church depended on the leadership and organization of the movement. In countries where State Churches existed, only a courageous person with boldness and leadership abilities was successful as an instrument for church growth within the State Church. A warm heart and diplomatic insight have characterized those who, by God's help, have succeeded in mobilizing some into the army of Jesus Christ.

The Western Inner Mission Association
(Det Vestlandske Indremisjonsforbund)

This society was successful in the Western part of Norway. In that area American and British church life had more influence than in the other areas of Norway. Emigrants, coming back to visit, brought new ideas with them to present in the old country. Hymns sung in the meetings of the Western Inner Mission Association were often born in America and in England.

The developments in this organization covered a long period. Hauge, Johnson, Rosenius and Traasdahl all had influenced the establishment of this society in 1898. Evangelism was directed from the headquarters that were located in Bergen. In the year of establishment, forty eight small societies from different locations were included. A great emphasis was laid on literature and educational ministry, though evangelism was always their main purpose. There was a very distinct line between believers and non-believers.

The Norwegian Lutheran Mission Society
(Det Norske Lutherske Misjonsamband)

Johannes Brandtzag was the founder of this organization. In 1891, it was born in the midst of the lay revival in Norway. In 1880-1890, a missionary revival swept the young people of Norway. Hudson Taylor and the China Inland Mission had an impact upon the believers. At that time the Norwegian Missionary Society (Det Norsk Misjonselskap, begun 1842) already existed. Many young people received a call to go to China as missionaries, but the mission school of the Norwegian Missionary Society was able only to take fifteen of the forty who had applied for candidacy. So some went to a mission field through a society in Great Britain or America (Aarflot, 1967: 456). Because of a need of training, this new organization sprang up. In 1890, sixteen societies in Rogaland joined the Norwegian Lutheran China Mission Association-- its original name (Det Norsk Luthersk Kinamisjonsforbund) changed in 1949 to the Norwegian Lutheran Mission Society (Det Norske Lutherske Misjonsamband).

Their purpose was not only for foreign missions, but also for evangelization at home. All activities were geared to evangelization. Throughout the country, 4,300 organizations joined the mission. About 230 lay preachers are presently active in Norway. They have sent out 200 missionaries to foreign lands.

The Laestadians in Norway

The Laestadian movement in Norway spread mostly in the northern part of the country. Because it gained most of its adherents from the Finnish-speaking people and the Lapps, we have included this movement with the Finnish awakening movements. There are few Laestadians in Norway outside Finnmark and Lappland.

In Norway, the Laestadians held anti-Church attitudes—which were later discouraged when they were connected with the State Church. In 1868, the Laestadians asked for permission to use the churches for their own meetings. They found that it was too disturbing and noisy when they worshipped with others who were not Laestadians. Two years later when permission was granted, the Laestadians also wished to have their own communion services. In 1887, nineteen years later, this became a reality when there were leadership changes in the Church of Norway.

Due to the separationist spirit in the Laestadian movement, it has not experienced much church growth and their territorial area has been limited. The lay leaders have had wisdom and insight regarding church growth. So they have handled the issues and tensions between them and the State Church tactfully.

Sweden

The Readers (Läsare)

Prior to the nineteenth century awakening in Sweden, the men who gave impetus to the awakening were outstanding: Henric Schartau (1757-1825), and Peter Lorentz Sellergren (1769-1843), and Peter Nyman (1794-1856); and also Lars Levi Laestadius (1800-1861), and Peter Wieselgren (1800-1877). Their fundamental messages stressed the moral demands of God.

There were different groups around the country without leadership in many cases. In 1820, George Scott, an English Methodist pastor, came to Sweden. He planned to minister to the British workers in Sweden but, when he saw how receptive the Swedes were, he learned their language and began preaching to them. Due to excessive drinking in the country he founded the first Christian Temperance Society in Sweden; he combined all the phases of the awakening movement: evangelism, temperance and colportage. Though Scott was a Methodist, he did not try to convert the Swedes to the Methodist point of view. Scott chose to present the Pietistic approach. His headquarters in Stockholm became the center of

the revival.   People came to hear him from far and near.
Many of the Lutheran ministers were in sympathy with Scott's
work. He also had many enemies, of course, who accused
him of secterian motives. In 1842, the opposition became so
strong that he had to flee the country.

A year before Scott fled the country, he met a young
Swede, Carl Olof Rosenius. Upon Scott's recommendation,
Rosenius was provided with a salary from America to do
evangelistic work in Sweden (Arden, 1964: 122).

The salary provision from America was by no means disturbing, for it was an international organization that was pro-
moting evangelism.   This was quite a common practice at
that time.   The arrangement gave Rosenius more opportunity
to travel in Sweden to spread the revival fires. Rosenius
took over Scott's church, Bethlehem Chapel in Stockholm,
and edited the periodical established in 1842. The 'Pietisten' issued a larger edition than the largest daily in Sweden
at one time.

The Readers got their name when the laymen started
to gather in homes to read the Bible. The rationalistic ideas
of the Enlightenment had influenced the ministers in the
churches. To meet their spiritual needs, the laymen began
to organize their own house meetings.

During the Readers' times, all private gatherings for
worship were banned by law, making arrest possible. This
law was not revoked until 1858. Sheriffs were urged by the
the State Church pastors to go to homes and arrest these
Readers.   The Pietists had a price to pay for their heart
religion. So many of them emigrated because they did not
have freedom of worship. A popular ditty of those days says:

>   I yearn for the country in the West,
>   For there they don't have any tormenting priests.

By the middle of the nineteenth century, it became necessary to organize all these small groups. So, in 1856, the
National Evangelical Foundation (Evangeliska Fosterlands-
stiftelsen) was formed. The purpose of the Foundation was
1) to promote and further the laymen's work in the revival;
2) to issue and distribute Christian literature. The Publishing house (which was founded in 1856) had printed more
than sixty-nine million pieces of literature by 1962.

The Swedish National Evangelical Foundation does not consider itself a free church. Rather it supplemented the work of the established State Church. The movement spread nation wide, and the strongest area of followers is in Västerbotten in Northern Sweden. Usually they tried to cooperate with the State Church in these areas by attending the morning divine services in the State Church. The evening meetings they hold in their own chapels and Prayer Houses, and these are usually evangelistic. Exceptions to this are the large cities like Stockholm where their work is carried on as independent congregations.

The movement carries on its own foreign mission work supporting about 125 missionaries. Their present membership in Sweden is about 30,000. Approximately 250 full-time preachers and 60 part-time workers are involved in the work of the Foundation.

The decline in their church growth during the last two decades has been partly due to the migration to large cities where it proves difficult to keep contact with the members.

Denmark

Grundtvigianism

Nicolai F. S. Grundtvig (1783-1872) was one of the three great Danes of the nineteenth century. The others were Hans Christian Andersen and Kierkegaard. Grundtvig made a great impact upon the Danish nation. It is necessary to understand Grundtvig himself in order to properly understand Grundtvigianism. He influenced both the intellectual and religious life of the country. He was a patriot. Arden says that he was the "most Danish Dane."

Grundtvig, after a great struggle, experienced a religious conversion in 1810. He had a desire to bring renewal to the Danes. He attracted many students and intellectuals to his services. To some extent, Grundtvig was inspired by Rousseau and the optimism of the Enlightenment. His theological views differed from those of the Pietists. The Grundtvigians were accused by the Pietists of being worldly. They did not stress conversion the same way as did the Pietists. Thus Grundtvig's motto: "Be human first, then a Christian," gave offense to many conservatives. Grundtvig stressed the view that a man is never isolated; he is always part of a real community (Hartling, 1964: 65).

Grundtvig was the father of the so-called free education known in the twentieth century in Scandinavia. He was dissatisfied with the theoretical-academic education. For this reason, he sought to add the practical aspect to education. For his work in establishing the folk schools of Denmark, a truly outstanding enterpise, Grundtvig is regarded as one of the world's great educationalists.

The period between 1825 and 1832 was probably the peak of Grundtvigianism (Thyssen, Vol. I: 150). Some adherents of Grundtvigianism formed their own free congregation after a split in the movement in 1832. This was because of their different theological views. However, the majority remained loyal with Grundtvig to the State Church. They were satisfied to get the best out of the State Church set-up.

Through the effort of the Grundtvigians, a new law came into power in 1855, which granted the liberty to join any other congregation. The members were no longer bound to their congregational geographic areas. If a minister from another congregation was willing to receive them, a move was in order.

Later on, another law came into operation that granted the privilege of starting a new congregation within the State Church, if this was the desire of at least twenty families. They had their own right to call a pastor and ask for permission to use State Church buildings (Hartling, 1964: 65).

Grundtvigianism had a special ministry for the intellectuals. Many ministers in the State Church joined the movement. From the church growth point of view, Grundtvigianism did not have much direct effect. Grundtvig pastored two congregations in Copenhagen: Our Saviour's and Vartov. The church attendances in his churches did not differ much from other congregations. (Thyssen, Vol. I:150) Some Grundtvig's disciples were engaged in a fight against the Baptists and tried to hinder their planting of churches in Denmark (Vol. I: 145). Hatred, opposition and persecution were the attitudes of Grundtvig and his followers towards the Baptists (Vol. I: 146).

The Association for the Inner Mission
(Forening for den Indre Misjon)

The Inner Mission was formed in the 1850s and was re-organized in 1861. Wilhelm Beck served as its chairman until 1901. He was known to be an effective and good organizer. Since many of the State Church ministers joined the mission, it remained in the existing church.

In the rural areas the Inner Mission was strongly Pietistic and emphasized conversion and sanctification. Laymen were engaged in witnessing and the distribution of literature in the country and these efforts helped the Inner Mission to progress more than in Copenhagen.

Nineteenth Century Copenhagen developed along the lines of social and philanthropic work. Due to industrialization the social problems in the city were great. The labor movement was not friendly towards the Church. The Church was regarded as an enemy of capitalism. Probably the Inner Mission tried to impress the laborers with their social work. Unfortunately this did not result in any church growth as much as in the rural areas where the laymen evangelized. The difference between the Grundtvigians and the Inner Mission was that the latter stressed immediate conversion while the former believed that one grows normally from infant baptism to becoming a Christian.

The Church Center Party
(Kirkeligt Centrum)

The Church Center Party does not have many adherents. It is a spiritual home of the clergy in Denmark. This work began under the leadership of Mynster and H. L. Martensen in 1899. Its purpose is to find new methods of evangelization. This movement has attracted people from various theological viewpoints.

Movements in the 20th Century

Prior to the 1905 Awakening in Wales, membership in the churches there was declining. The desperate situation was recognized by leaders of the Churches, and a spiritual revival was said to be the supreme need (Orr, 1968: 1). Once the expected revival had begun, the leaders involved were confident that it would spread all over the world. It penetrated Great Britain, Scandinavia, most of Europe, North and Latin America, India, the Orient and Africa. Evan Roberts' vision was fulfilled in that hundreds of thousands were won for the Lord and added to the Church at large.

The 1905 Awakening in Scandinavia

Before the Welsh Revival began, the Lord had prepared the ground in Scandinavia. Count Moltke in 1900 had invited members of various denominations to his home for prayer meetings. The impact was so powerful that public prayer meetings resulted. Similar desire for prayer was reported in Sweden and Norway. In 1903, a week of prayer in Stockholm produced an ingathering as young converts sought a church home (Orr, 1969: 59).

In Denmark, Wilhelm Beck, who had witnessed the awakening of 1860s (Thyssen, 1961, Vol. II: 107, 175), took a stand against the drunkenness and immorality among State Church clergy. In 1902, local revivals occurred on the two main islands of Denmark. The following years witnessed a great impact upon Danish youth. Prayer meetings were well-attended by the young people. In the fall of 1905, the news of the awakening in Wales had reached every part of Denmark, and 'pentecostal winds' swept the country. A State Church minister, H. P. Møllerup, preached nightly to overflowing audiences in Denmark's largest hall, in Copenhagen. Revival songs were heard in the streets of the capital, whose whole atmosphere was cleansed. Other parts of Denmark saw the same kind of results.

This early twentieth century awakening resulted in the birth of the Danish Young People's Society in the State Church. A State Church worker reported to the Inner Mission: "We have had a marvelous winter this year. . . There has not been a winter like this since Christianity came to our country " (Orr, 1968: 64).

In Norway, the theological controversy at the beginning of the century had caused a decline in church attendance. Then in 1904 an earthquake occurred in Norway, shaking some people and reminding them of the uncertainty of earthly life. A few months later, a spiritual awakening shook people everywhere. Nothing like it had been seen since the days of Hans Nielsen Hauge. The awakening was interdenominational in character. The instrument that God greatly used was Albert Lunde, an ex-seaman converted in America. Lunde carried an extraordinary burden for revival and, after hearing of the revival in Wales, he gained much encouragement. Lunde was sound in doctrine and diplomatically skillful in his relations with the State Church of Norway. Permission was given him to preach in the State Churches, and his work was supported by State Church clergy. In 1905, Lunde preached to crowds of 5000 and more in Oslo (Orr, 1968: 62). The revival was felt in all social classes except the upper strata which were slow to humble themselves before God. Menighetsfakultet, an independent School of Theology within the State Church, was founded as a result of this awakening. It led ministers and laymen to deeper commitment and faithfulness.

In Sweden, the awakening followed the Norwegian pattern. Norway and Sweden were then a united kingdom, but tensions were felt between the two nations. Despite this, the news of revival in Oslo impelled the Swedes to invite Albert Lunde to Stockholm to preach in the great auditorium, Blasieholm-kyrkan. The meetings were attended by royalty and by commonality. The whole country was swept by the revival. Another movement began within the year at Philadelphia Chapel, Stockholm (Orr, 1968: 66). Special prayer meetings were organized by ministers in the Swedish capital, and all denominations took part in them in large numbers. The awakening created a greater interest in missions, growth in church membership, and a change for the better in society.

In Finland, the awakening of 1905 appeared not to have had as great an impact as in the other Scandinavian lands, perhaps due to troubles with Russian imperialism. Revivals in various parts of the country were reported. One began among the Swedish-speaking Finns in the Aland islands and on the west coast of Finland. Among the Finnish-speaking Finns, the awakening was known as Hannula's Revival, after a missionary named Frans Hannula traveled across the country in mission meetings. Young people in particular were drawn to the meetings (Haavio, 1965: 89-90). Prayer houses were built. Witnesses of this revival related that in eastern Finland cries for mercy were heard and people fell on the floor in an agony of conviction of sin (Orr, 1968: 67).

Hannula's Revival tended to become an independent work, but through careful handling it later merged with the State Church. Haavio in his study noted that even half a century later there were ten rectors in the State Church who made reference to the impact of Hannula's Revival (1965: 90).

The Later 20th Century

Since that time, this century has not seen any awakenings which could compare to those of the nineteenth century in Scandinavia. The Christian faith has been attacked by communist ideology, secularization and industrialization. Only Finland and Norway have been fortunate to see some fruit from the last century awakenings. In Finland, post-war movements have been organized and we will now deal with them individually.

The Inner Mission Foundation (Sisälähetyssäätiö)

Behind the Inner Mission Foundation there is a personality as in other evangelical movements. Urho Muroma, a Lutheran minister, was one of the most outstanding preachers in the twentieth century. We can trace the influences of Muroma's lifework to two sources, the Lutheran Pietism and the Anglo-American Evangelicalism.

Though Muroma did not favor any of the major awakening movements in the Church of Finland, he wanted to use the best out of them all in his life and preaching (Hakalisto, 1966: 14) The Lutheran Pietism gave the theological basis for his work and the Anglo-American Evangelicalism had a great influence on Muroma's evangelistic techniques.

A Norwegian revival preacher, Albert Lunde, was instrumental in Moroma's conversion in 1912 when he was preaching in the Lutheran State Church in Helsinki. While Muroma was ordained in the Lutheran Church, the duties of a State Church pastor never attracted him. The reason for this, he said, was: "their secular emphasis and lack of evangelistic concern " (Vanha-Perttula, 1949:136).

Muroma could well be called the father of the modern revival movement in Finland. His sermons were strongly Biblical. He moved the hearts of common men by his colloquial illustrations. Muroma had the courage to stand against the elite in Finland. He was the watchman over the Israel in Finland. As a man of patriotism, he continued to preach in spite of public opposition and ridicule. Those who consciously tried to weaken the nation's morals and its powers of resistance, no matter how civilized and elite they were, Muroma called them "traitors of the fatherland " (Honkanen, 1967: 95).

As a true shephard, Muroma guarded the flock of believers in Finland against liberal influences from Sweden, especially in the decade 1950-1960.

The revival in which Muroma was instrumental reached its peak in 1920-1930. During this period, a series of meetings would last two or three weeks in one place. As a result of this revival in Finland, the Inner Mission Foundation, which also sponsors its own Bible Institute, was born in 1940. The motives for starting the School were:

1) The Bible knowledge of the Christians was poor.
2) Too many Christians suffered from under nourished spiritual lives.
3) The new converts were in danger of false prophets, their scripture knowledge being poor (Kankainen, 1967: 186).

The care of the new Christians was important to Muroma. He wanted to train the laymen in the Church of Finland in an effective way to propagate their faith. Another important aspect of this ministry was the provision of literature. There

was a need for evangelical literature in the Finnish language.
He wrote several books and articles and was the founder and
editor of the Herää Valvomaan magazine, for the purpose of
leading believers into a deeper spiritual life.

It was Muroma's aim to cooperate with the existing State
Church and its ministers. He went to speak in parishes only
upon official invitation. As this Foundation works within the
State Church, it does not have any members. The only way
to estimate their adherents is through the regular financial
contributors, which were as follows:

1950 - 3468
1955 - 5643
1960 - 8468
1965 - 8566
1969 - 7435

The loss of supporters after 1965 was caused by the organization of a new movement in Finland in 1967, designated
Finland's Folkmission, (Suomen Kansanlähetys).

In 1967, the Bible Institute had about 800 groups of
"friends" around the country. It is difficult to estimate the
exact number because these groups are known only when
they send in their financial support. Three laymen under
the leadership of a minister visited these groups and 198
meetings for evangelism were held during the year, 1967.
Days spent at Bible Institutes numbered 29; meetings for
"friends" 83; and other meetings, 521 (Evankelisluterilaisen, 1968:8). The Inner Mission Foundation also has
a tape ministry.   Most of Urho Muroma's sermons and
Bible studies were taped. These are lent to the various
supporters or "friends." It is impossible to estimate how
many persons listen to these tapes.

To some degree, the Inner Mission Foundation has influenced most of the congregations of the State Church. The
death of the founder was one of many reasons why the effective vitality of this Foundation has not lasted long. It has
become very Churchly and is careful not to cause any dis-
turbance in the Church of Finland. The more extensive educational emphasis has slowed down their church growth.
Maybe the Foundation would have done better, from the
church growth aspect, if it had been more aggressive in

evangelizing.   Lack of opposition seemed to cause a spiritual leveling off in Finland.

People's Bible Society (Kansan Raamattuseura)

The People's Bible Society was born as a fruit of the Frank Mangs' revival in 1945. At that time there was a lack of Bibles in Finland, and the purpose of the society was to supply God's Word to the new converts.

Frank Mangs was a Finn from the Swedish-speaking part of Finland. He became the Billy Graham of Scandinavia. In the middle of World War I, he received his call to preach. Due to the troublous times in Finland, he was not able to complete his education, but started to preach. Mangs was especially gifted as an evangelist. More than any other evangelist in Scandinavia, he was a counselor. Mangs said that he had never heard so many confessions as he heard during the Finnish winter war. Revival swept across the country, and included all classes and all age groups. All denominations worked together in good understanding. Churches were too small to hold all the people who wanted to come to church. Talvitie (1957) says that Christianity never influenced young people more than during Mangs's revival. The population of the cities was evacuated often during the war, so the new converts carried the revival fires with them to the countryside.

Most of the people who came to church were women, because it was war time and the men were at the Front. Mangs realized this and went there where the men were fighting at the Russian border, and preached to them.

Mangs's success can be credited to the great receptivity during the war. He was a true Finn, a lover of fatherland, and had the heart of a counselor. No one else seemed to understand the suffering and problems which the Finns were going through both as a nation and as individuals. One wonders if proper care had been given the converts, in shepherding them, would there have been better churchgrowth results?

The People's Bible Society is not typically Finnish since it has been influenced by the Free Church movement. It is not an opposition movement. The State Church welcomes its over twenty full-time workers to hold meetings in its churches. Yearly, the People's Bible Society has about 300 series of evangelistic meetings. Some of them are held in the State Churches, where its workers go only when invited; others are held in tents during the summer time.

In 1969, the Society had seven camping centers. There are held the young people's confirmation camps. This is a service that they render to the State Church. In this way the young people would not be exposed to a minister who perhaps would not be born again, but would receive vital Christian truth and teaching instead. The Society's special emphasis was on confession, forgiveness and conversion. About a quarter of its full-time workers are engaged in various Lutheran congregations. The Foundation has a special ministry to young people and students. They do not have members, but the camping centers have regular supporters, though there are not any statistics available.

The Helsinki Bible School Foundation
(Helsingin Raamattukoulun Säätiö)

Early in this century, Liberalism took hold of many of the churches in Scandinavia and spread to the theological schools and university faculties. This concept produced many liberally minded ministers in the churches. Liberalism denied the Bible truths. It was with this background that the Bible School Foundation began its work in Finland, 1953, to fill an urgent need.

Kerttu Vaininkainen, a deaconess in the State Church of Finland related that she began to read the Bible with the sole purpose of finding out what was wrong in it. She studied the Bible several times from cover to cover. In 1928, when she was reading her Bible as usual, she came to Leviticus, chapter sixteen, the story of the great redemption day. This passage opened the secrets of the Bible to her and she found Christ through the Old Testament. This experience resulted in the birth of the Bible School idea in Finland.

After a period of preparation and study on the continent, Kerttu Vaininkainen returned to Finland with a determination to start teaching the Bible to the public. A small newspaper advertisment informed the public in Helsinki of this opportunity. Vainikainen expected only about twenty to come to the small chapel in the State Church, but one hundred and forty persons turned up. This was exactly seven times more than she had prayed for. This was the confirmation that she needed to know God was pleased with her plan. (Vainikainen, 1968)

In the beginning, the Bible School Foundation had school activities in the evenings only, using the State Church buildings. The clergy were not always understanding about this, and suggested they buy property. One of the great problems in Finland is to get property at a reasonable price. The Foundation bought two apartments in the city, which served as meeting rooms. The opportunity for evening meetings was limited because of the near neighbors. Singing and any music also had to be left out for the same reason.

Financially, the Foundation is dependent on free will offerings of the people. Tithing and sacrificial giving is entirely new to the State Church people, who already pay taxes to the Church. This matter of giving has taken a long time to mature among the Finnish Christians, and this has been a barrier to the furtherance of the Gospel in the independent groups within the State Church.

The Bible School Foundation does not have members as such. It has "friends," regular financial supporters. It has drawn people to study the Bible from all social classes, although the majority are from the middle class. In addition to the Bible Studies held at the Helsinki property, there are regular evening Bible Schools open to the public in other major cities. Whenever they are invited, the Foundation has meetings for the State Church congregations.

The period 1960-1967 was especially fruitful in evangelistic work. Many young people studied there for full-time Christian service. Some opposition from the State Church and financial difficulties made the Foundation more reliant upon God. In 1966 the training for professional evangelists and youth leaders was recognized and accredited by the State Church. This year was the turning point in the success of the Foundation. The accreditation involved many non-essential subjects for evangelistic training. It limited much of its evangelistic liberty and outreach. The full-time lay evangelists were advised to be careful in their evangelistic approach in the Church.

The year 1967 brought many crises on the evangelistic frontier in the State Church. One stream was aggressively evangelistic. Contrary to the leaders in the independent movements, they wanted to have the whole church as their missionfield. They were not satisfied to go there only when invited. If a certain congregation refused their request to hold meetings in their area, these evangelistically minded laymen and some clergy as well would go anyway and put up their tent and invite people to come to Christ.

The year 1967 closed with the result that most of the evangelists employed by the Bible School Foundation, realized that cooperation was impossible without compromising their call and vision. There was a loss of personnel and many of the "friends" of the Foundation witheld their contributions.

The Bible School Foundation had educated, all told, about 120 full-time youth leaders and evangelists in the church, and about 250 non-professionals who have studied the Bible verse by verse from cover to cover. The Bible School Foundation is continuing on the principle that it give the Bible into the hands of the people, who can experience its teachings in their everyday life.

Finland's People's Mission (Suomen Kansanlähetys)

This movement is the newest in Finland. Its date of organization was 1967. The idea for this kind of mission was in the minds of the evangelicals in the country, for a long time. They felt that it had become difficult to evangelize unbelievers in the State Church, because of the opposition and closed doors they met in the State Church.

The purpose of the People's Mission, with the Lutheran doctrine as its base, is to evangelize people so that they will evangelize others. They believe in the unity of believers. Every believer is to be guided and trained to serve Christ using the spiritual gifts that God has given to each one. The inner mission or the home mission is the responsibility of

local believers. They are taught to evangelize their own community. Short training sessions for laymen are provided during the weekends to make them qualified for soulwinning. The People's Mission also emphasizes the importance of small prayer groups gathering in private homes.

Evangelistic meetings are held in the State Church properties, where the leadership is friendly toward this new movement. It has expanded rapidly among the youth and those evangelisticly minded people coming mainly from the Bible School of Helsinki and the Inner Mission Foundation supporters.

The movement does not have members. It is comparable to the Norwegian Lutheran Mission Society in its aim and work. In 1967 the People's Mission had ten full-time workers and now, in 1970, they have sixty-five. The adherents can be estimated by the subcription list of the "Uusi Tie", the weekly magazine of the evangelically minded Lutherans in Finland. In 1967 "Uusi Tie" had 11,000 subcriptions and by 1970 there are 17,000 (Väliaho, 1970). Several adherents may be reading the same paper.

When the movement was organized, it was noticeable that the mission interest was great among the young people. The Finnish Lutheran Mission Society was known to be "high church." Some of the young people who had a call to be missionaries, could not be accepted in the Mission School, because they did not have academic education or some professional competence such as a teacher, nurse or engineer, etc. Pastor Väisänen, one of the leaders in the People's Mission said that when he traveled across the country in 1967, about fifty young people had expressed their desire to go to to the missionfield, if the Lord would open the door for them. In 1969 these junior candidates numbered about 500 (Väisänen, 1969).

The People's Mission bought a property in 1968 in Ryttylä, sixty miles from Helsinki. This has been popularly called the "Ryttylä Miracle," because, through God's providence, they were able to buy thirty acres of land and several buildings suitable for a mission school, faculty houses and dormitories, all for the price of a private home. In October, 1969, the Mission School and Center was dedicated. In 1970 the school has sixty-three students.

The financial support is arranged through "faith pledges." Every believer is encouraged to send in their monthly tithes. The People's Mission has awakened among the people a tremendous desire to share their belongings and give sacrificially for the sake of evangelism at home and on the foreign fields. The missionaries who are sent out by the People's Mission go to fields supervised by the Norwegian Lutheran Mission Society. Small groups of believers at home support their respective missionaries financially. The ideal is for the group of local believers, from whom the missionary comes, to support him or her.

In less than three years the movement has spread almost across the whole country. Sixteen regional organizations have been founded. They operate the same way as the free churches in America. The People's Mission practises the Church Growth principles more than any other church or movement in Finland. It is completely self-governing; self propagating and self-supporting. Should cooperation with the State Church become impossible in the future, it will be able to continue as a free church.

Renewal Movements Fostering Free Churches

The Readers

The movement which produced the Readers in various parts of Scandinavia gave birth to several permanent organizations throughout the northern lands. Their success added to the strength of the Free Churches.

The Mission Covenant Church
(Svenska Missionsförbundet)

The Swedish Mission Covenant Church is the oldest and largest of all the Mission Covenant Churches in the union of such organizations throughout Scandinavia. A strong Bible Readers' Movement in Sweden was first formed through the National Evangelical Foundation, which was closely affiliated with the State Church. In 1878, some of the adherents felt that the ties with the State Church were too strong and broke away.

The central figure in the Swedish Mission Covenant was Paul Peter Waldenström (1838-1917). He took over after Carl Olof Rosenius the editorship of the periodical "Pietisten," which had become the most influential religious periodical in all of Sweden. Paul Peter Waldenström was a noted scholar and a spiritual leader in the Bible Readers' movement. In 1872, his doctrine of atonement was published, and shook the Church. It taught that God's anger was not aroused over the sins of men. Waldenström did not hold it necessary that the Atonement was the provision for righteousness. He was soon labeled an anti-Christ. In conservative groups, this was just as serious an error as the doctrine denying Christ's divinity. Other doctrinal questions, Holy Communion and baptism, were burning issues among believers in Sweden. No doubt these controversial issues were also used for polemics and the winning of people to the new movement.

Free Church Views

The Mission Covenant people wanted most of all to be just good Lutherans, but wanted to be free in non-essential doctrine. The State Church and later the Pentecostalists were against the founding of a new denomination (Nyhlen 1964:109). The Mission Covenant people were guided by the fact that at least two uses of the term "the Church of Christ" occurred in the New Testament:

     a. The communion of the saints (i.e., believers)

     b. The local congregation of believing Christians.

The Christian congregation, in the latter sense, comes into existence when believers unite for mutual edification, discipline and aid, as well as for the work of extending the Kingdom of God (Olson, 1964:201).

The following are the guides for church growth:

1) The membership in the church is open to all who confess Christ as personal Saviour.

2) The members are free to stay as members in the "prestige church" i.e. in the State Church, if they so desire. This saves them from embarrassment among their families. Then they would not be considered as disloyal. The Mission Covenant Church is their spiritual home and the State Church serves as a civilian organization, as a state registry.

3) The unity of believers is to be strongly stressed.

4) The work in the church is to be well organized.

5) The pioneering leaders, Waldenström as the spiritual leader and J. E. Ekman as an organizer, as these laid good foundations for the church from the beginning.

The Mission Covenant Church in Norway
(Den Norsk Misjons Fǿrbund)

The Mission Covenant Church in Norway was founded in 1884. The influences of Hauge, Lammers and Franson made a great impact upon the new union. Hauge fought for the right of laymen, Lammers for the right of believers to establish a free church (Olson 1964:170 - 176) and Franson introduced Moody's methods of evangelism.

Franson was a successful church planter. In the thirteen months he was in Norway, he established twelve churches (1964:176). The interest in foreign missions grew and many young people volunteered themselves for the foreign field.

The church growth results of Franson's visit were:

1) The church met a need in Norway by gathering "homeless" believers.

2) The leaders had good personal contact with the different societies.

3) A nation-wide revival including all the classes, through the ministry of the Finnish evangelist, Frank Mangs, in the 1930s. The war contributed favorably to the church growth in the 1940s.

The Mission Covenant Church of Denmark
(Det Dansk Misjonsførbund)

The Danish Mission Covenant Church stems from the revival in the nineteenth century. The Inner Mission and the visits of Hans Nielsen Hauge laid the foundation for this organization. The example set by Sweden in the attempt to build free churches was so encouraging that the believers in Denmark wanted to follow in the same steps.

Jens Jensen-Maar

Jensen-Maar was a member of the Danish Inner Mission. He was warned about false prophets; the free church minded believers preaching in Denmark. However a woman preacher Catherine Juell, impressed Jensen-Maar so much, that he decided to join the independent movement. This was why he was later expelled from the Inner Mission. Jensen-Maar had held sincere loyalty to the State Church, but he decided to do what he felt was God's will.

The new Mission Covenant Church, founded officially in 1888, had the set purpose of uniting believers only in a fellowship to propagate the Gospel at home and abroad. There were Church Growth lessons:

1) The first ten years of history of the Mission Covenant in Denmark was marked with revival. The Church was vital.

2) In 1912, some of the believers wanted to go all the way with Christ in the Church. The holiness emphasis came with Erik Anderson from Norway. It resulted in schism in the Church in Denmark. Although the purpose of the Mission Covenant Union was to welcome all "regardless of doctrinal views," the holiness people were not welcome. Naturally there was much one-sided emphasis and failure in the holiness people, but this is common of every individual and movement at the beginning of a new experience. It is possible that the Mission Covenant Church in Denmark made a big mistake by rejecting the holiness message early in the century. Anderson's congregation in Oslo became the starting point of the Pentecostal movement in Norway (Olson 1964 : 229). God blessed His work anyway.

3) In 1935 Nyland's Mission was organized for better evangelization in Denmark. House meetings and Gospel tent meetings were held. In spite of many efforts the growth of the Church has remained very small. Even though there are many church activities, the church lacks spiritual vitality and warmth.

The Free Evangelical Churches of Finland
(Fria Missionsförbundet; Suomen Vapaakirkko)

The Mission Covenant Church in Finland was founded in 1889. In some circles in the State Church there was a tendency towards the free church ideas. It expressed itself in their having separate Holy Communion to the others in the State Church. This aroused an interest of the English Lord Radstock, who visited in Finland in 1889. Being of noble birth, Radstock made a great impact upon the nobility in Russian Finland. He was instrumental in bringing an awakening to the Czar Alexander II's household in Leningrad. Colonel Paschkoff opened his palace for evangelistic meetings to which the nobility were invited and as a result many of them were converted (Salmensaari, 1957:44).

Radstock had a great influence upon the upper class. He usually spoke in languages of prestige, French and English. On his evangelistic travels he took along his wife, seven children and several servants. An evangelist, living in the most expensive hotels, impressed the upper class people. Most of his audiences came from these exclusive circles (Salmensaari, 1957:45-46).

The key person, however, was Constantin Boije of Gennäs, also a member of the nobility. He was sent to Leningrad to school where he was awakened to his spiritual needs. When he wanted to consult a minister of the church, he was denied this opportunity. At the age of nineteen Boije went to Sweden to the Mission School of the National Evangelistic Foundation. In Sweden, his contact with the Free Church followers resulted in his being forced to leave the Lutheran School (Salmensaari, 1957:37).

Returning to Finland, Boije began evangelistic activities with Jakob Forsberg. In spite of opposition, an awakening was experienced in many places. In 1883 Boije founded the first free church in Helsinki (1957:39). The State Church clergy and police did all they could to stop these meetings. Both Boije and Forsberg were supported by the Swedish Mission Covenant in the early years in Finland.

In 1889, the Dissenters' Law permitted the founding of religious associations based on the Bible. Complete religious freedom was granted in 1923. One of the free church leaders Edw. Björkenheim, told the annual meeting in 1896 that the State Church was forcing them out of the church. They used the children of the free church people as a means to accomplish their plans. As the children were not recorded in the church registers, they were the object of persecution when they were in school. In the Finnish society the State Church would not use harsh means in attacking the free church. (1957:210)

Tension between the Different Homogeneous Units

The real reason why the Swedish speaking Fria Missionsförbundet separated from the Finnish was the tension between the two language groups and not the organization. With the language differences there were national feelings, differences in education and two different views on missions (Salmensaari, 1957:253). By 1920 the Finnish speaking group already outnumbered the Swedish speaking. Since the mission

began in the Swedish language, the Swedish speaking people
wanted to continue in that language. Separation between these
two homogeneous units took place in 1922.

Church growth lessons learned are as follows:

1) The Mission Covenant in Finland has not had any outstanding leading personalities, and this has benefitted the
church growth among them. It has given more flexible
views, and it has not been narrowed down to one person's
convictions and principles.

2) The separation between the homogeneous units: the Finnish speaking side records remarkable church growth after
the separation. The reason for the slow growth among the
Swedish was that they depended too much on the help from
the Swedish sister church. Their preachers were not willing
to learn Finnish. They were unwilling to go to the responsive
rural areas. The Swedish speaking people considered themselves a more prestigious people. To be accepted by them
one had to meet certain linguistic, educational and class requirements.

3) The free church was friendly towards the State Church.
It offers formal membership to those belonging to the State
Church. This, however, does not give the right to vote in
board meetings.

4) The free church used neutral meeting halls for their services, and had house meetings.

5) In the beginning of its history, a holiness emphasis rose
among the free church people. The majority felt, however,
this was being too religious, and the fire was soon put out.

6) The "Billy Graham of Scandinavia," Frank Mangs, a Finnish born evangelist, was preaching in Finland with results
in awakening and church growth.

The Baptists in Scandinavia

As early as the 1550's Anabaptist revivals have been recorded in Denmark (Jensen 1960:27). In 1734 about ninety
Swedes and Finns came to Copenhagen seeking a better living.
They had strong Baptist views and were influential for revival in the city. After a few months' stay, they received permission to go to Frederica where there was more religious

liberty. However, the State Church priests rose up against them. No one in Frederica was willing to take them in. A woman even had to give birth to a child out in the cold winter (Jensen 1961: 29).

Baptists in Denmark

It took one hundred years before the first Baptist church was organized in Copenhagen in 1839. Then the first nine persons were baptized and the first free church in Denmark was founded (1961:35). The Baptist candidates gathered outside at 6 p.m. After kneeling in prayer, testimonies were given; then the women were baptized first and then the men (Thyssen, 1960:121-2).

Peter Christian Mønster (1797-1870) became the first leader in the Baptist church in Copenhagen, and in 1843 there were 100 members---74 men and 26 women. They were mostly young people; the average age was 28-29 years (Thyssen: 135-6). By 1844, the membership had grown to 321, and by 1850 it was 360 (1960:135-6).

Mønster had trouble with the authorities and was arrested several times. An English woman, Elizabeth Fry, visited Denmark and through her visits and letters to the Danish King, Christian VIII, she was influential in getting more religious liberty for the country (1961:96-98). Other churches in England and America presented a petition to the Danish King and requested religious freedom for their brothers in the faith. The persecution against the Baptists was so strong that many Danes emigrated to other countries. The Danish colonies in India were said to have more liberty than free church people in Denmark (1960:124). They were not allowed to invite any who were not already members to the meetings. The Baptists, however, broke these rules and continued to take new members by baptism. They were even denied freedom to speak or sing at the grave yard without permission from the State Church priest! (1960:132-4).

The State Church in Denmark continued to enforce infant baptism. A State Church priest would come, accompanied by the police, to get the children of Baptists, and force them into their church where they were baptized. A son of Peder

Larsen, when he was eleven and a half years old, got so scared at the State Church christening that he died. A son of Højer became so sick when forcibly baptized that he died the next day (Jensen 1961:116). The Rev. P.C. Kierkegaard, brother of Søren Kierkegaard, was the first pastor in the State Church not to want to baptize Baptist children by force (1961: 117).

Hindrances to church growth in the Baptist churches in Denmark included the Mormons, who came to Scandinavia at the beginning of 1900. At that time, there were about 30,000 Danish Mormons already in America. They influenced their relatives in Scandinavia. The Baptists lost many members to the Mormons, who took over the harvest which ardent Baptists had planted.

Baptists in Sweden

The first people (four men and one woman in Borekulla, Halland) to turn to the Baptists were baptized in 1848. The preacher was a Danish born Baptist minister, E. M. Förster, sent to Sweden from Hamburg. About the same time a Swedish born Baptist preacher, Frederik Olaus Nilsson, began to preach. A year later the first Baptist church in Sweden had 50 members (Nyhlen, 1964: 141). The persecution from the State Church priests was so strong that in 1853, Nilsson and 21 other Baptists had to leave Sweden and go to America. Nilsson returned to Sweden secretly in 1860; by then, there were already 4500 members in Baptist churches (1964:142).

At the time of the first Baptist Conference, 45 churches and 2105 members were reported. In the beginning the work was mostly supported from America. Due to the persecution it was hard to get sufficient finances for the Baptist mission. By 1866, American-sponsored preachers in Sweden sold or distributed 42,000 books, 332,000 tracts (Nyhlen,1964:147).

The period 1882-87 proved to be the most successful in Baptist history in Sweden. During that time, 21,000 were baptized. The peak in membership was reached in 1929 before the great schism which took place in the 1930s. John Ongman, acquainted with the Holiness Movement in America and influenced by it, still preferred to stay with the Baptist fellowship. After Ongman's death in 1931, the younger generation wanted freedom, which resulted in an open separation in 1936. The formal Baptist denomination lost seventy of their congregations to the new Orebro Mission Association which theologically was ranked between Baptist and Pentecostal, structurally more like the Pentecostals. No statistics are kept of their outreach. In 1964, they had 200 churches and 25,000 members (Nyhlen, 1964: 173).

One reason for the schism in the 1930s (and at the beginning of this century when the Free Baptists separated from the mother church taking 7,000 members with them) was their loose organization. The Baptists have lost many of their members to the Pentecostal movement, and to the Örebro Mission Association of charismatic Baptists.

Baptists in Finland

The Baptist mission work in Finland began with Swedish speaking Finns in the 1850s. The first group of Baptist believers were found in Föglö in 1856. The movement found adherents on the West coast, who were also Swedish speaking. The first Finnish speaking Baptist work was organized in Luvia in 1870 (Haavio, 1965:141). At the turn of the century the two language groups separated into independent organizations. The Baptists then had 2800 members in ten churches.

The growth of the Baptist cause reached its peak during World War I; then the connection had about 5,000 members. After the war, the membership went down to below 2,000 (1965: 142).

The reason for poor growth seems to be that the Baptist churches did not really meet the real need of the Finns. The Finnish speaking people had their own awakening movements in the State Church. They were in the Finnish language and of several varieties. After World War I came, many other radical movements began in Finland that won more adherents. This is probably one of the reasons why the Baptists had such a great loss in membership.

Baptists in Norway

A Danish missionary, Fredrik L. Rymker (1819-84),

founded the first Baptist church in Norway in 1850. Members came from Porsgrunn and Skien, evangelistic centers in the south of Norway.

In 1863, Rymker went back to Denmark. A Norse seaman, G. Hübert (1829-1901), who had been converted in America, quietly continued the Baptist work which Rymker had begun. Hübert founded a church in Bergen and, during a ten year period, four other churches were formed. In 1879, when the Baptist movement in Norway took form as a Union, there were between fourteen and eighteen churches.

The Methodists in Scandinavia

The Methodist Church in Scandinavia remains faithful to Wesley's structural organization of his church. It has its own bishops and hierarchy, and had its best success in Norway, where the religious climate was warm. In comparison to the others, the Norwegians have been the most active of all the Scandinavian Methodist Churches in evangelism. In the other three countries, Denmark, Sweden and Finland, the Methodist Church is so much like the State Church with its formality that it has not made any mentionable impact on the people of the northern countries.

The Methodists in Sweden

George Scott, whom we have already mentioned earlier in connection with the Readers movement, was sent to Sweden to organize the Methodist church. Scott formed a church but the Holy Spirit led the revival movement that was going on in different ways, and the Church developed a completely different form, not labeled the Methodist Church.

Some Swedish seamen who were converted in New York had been Methodists in America. Small groups of Methodists sprang up in the American manner, when they visited their home country. Scott, who had earlier promised his friends there would not be any Methodist church in Sweden, (Nyhlen, 1964:203) now warned them against the American Methodists.

Victor Witting (1825-1905) was the most significant in spreading Methodism in Sweden. He was one of those who had been converted in America and had returned to his country in 1867 when he was asked by Bishop Kingsley to be the leader of the Methodist work in Sweden. Witting was sponsored by the American Methodists, and his contacts across the Atlantic helped him finance the new work. The efforts of Witting were blessed by revival which greatly inspired the friends in America. A year later, Witting was able to get a printing press as a help to lead the new converts to a deeper spiritual life.

At the beginning of the twentieth century, the interest of the Methodists was directed to social work. At this time, the Pentecostal movement was making an impact on Swedish soil. The Methodists lost many members to Pentecostalism.

The present problems of the Methodists in Sweden, as well as in other Scandinavian countries, are that the vast majority of members are old people who cannot attend church regularly. The Methodist Church is known as a dying Church in Sweden.

The tragedy is more noticeable when the Church is small. The definite weakness of the Methodist Church has been its external structural likeness to that of the State Church. The Methodists have lost many of its ministers to the State Church, where there has been more prestige and better pay. Since the Wesleyan doctrine of holiness is not much emphasized anymore, the transfer to the State Church has been an easy one.

The Methodists in Norway

A Norwegian seaman, Ole P. Petersen from Fredrikstad (1822-1901), brought Methodism to Norway. Having been converted in New York, he began to testify about his experience to his people. His simple but powerful testimony brought revival to many. A year later, Petersen received an invitation to come to Iowa to evangelize the Scandinavian immigrants there. After his ordination in the Methodist Church in 1853, however, Petersen settled in Norway again. The first Methodist church was formed there in 1856 and had 43 members, the Methodist first-fruits in Norway.

In the 1880s, there was an extensive geographical expansion; 24 churches were planted. By 1905 the Methodist Church in Norway had 45 churches. In 1969 the Methodists numbered 11,342, which is the largest membership of all the Methodist churches in Scandinavia   (Aarflot, 1967: 380).

The Methodists in Finland

Following the same pattern as in the other Scandinavian countries, a seaman brought Methodism back to Finland in the 1860s. The first unofficial church was founded in Vaasa among the Swedish speaking Finns in 1881. The work among the Finnish speaking people began in the 1890s. Its evangelization has concentrated upon the cities, rather than the countryside.

From the start, they won middle and upper class people. The Church in Finland reached its peak in 1930. Formalism caused the decline. The Methodist meetings in Finland, so far have never drawn crowds.   The Church came as a package deal to Scandinavia. The followers of Wesley, with such a fine message and theology, have been completely handicapped in Finland, because of the hierarchical church structure, inherited from the American Methodists from the early nineteenth century denominational pattern.

The present membership of the Swedish speaking Methodist Church in Finland is 1,099, and the Finnish speaking church has 924 members. The majority are old people. The church has its theological school in Göteborg, Sweden. In 1968, the School which serves all four Scandinavian countries had 24 students, 15 from Norway, 4 from Sweden and 1 from Denmark as well as 4 from Finland. Three students from Finland are Swedish speaking   (MSVKV. 1969).

The Finnish speaking Methodist Church, especially, has weak leadership. All through its existence, it has been like a child, expecting financial assistance from the wealthy "American Uncle." The hierarchy of the Church guarantees the salaries of the clergy and living quarters. Hierarchy, formalism, financial security, and foreign assistance have produced a dead monument to Methodism in Finland, as else where in Scandinavia.

The Methodists in Denmark

The Methodist Church was organized in Denmark in 1859. The one instrument responsible for this was a Danish immigrant, Christian Willerup, who was converted to Methodism in New York. Willerup's application for government recognition of the Methodist church in Denmark, was granted in 1865, thus making the religious services legal. The Methodists began their welfare work in the 1920s, and this resulted in their neglecting evangelism. The membership dropped considerably. The peak in membership was in 1920 when they had 4,858 members. In 1969 the membership was 3,232. The Methodist spirit can be described with the words of the Rev. Eigil Carlsen (Hartling 1964:138) who said that the Methodist Church in Denmark "has made its contribution to Danish Church life, and its influence has been considerable, especially on philanthropic and welfare work."

Scandinavian Pentecostals

Pentecostalism came to Scandinavia from America where T.B. Barratt had visited and become acquainted with the new revival. Before going to America, Barratt served as a Methodist pastor in Norway. In 1902 Barratt started an independent City Mission in Oslo (Kristiania). The purpose of his American trip was to collect money for his mission in Norway (Block-Hoell 1964:66-67). This journey, however, was not as successful as he had wished; sometimes he had to go without meals. Barratt received something better than money for he heard news of the Pentecostal revival in Los Angeles. He was baptized by the Spirit in one meeting in New York—and spoke in tongues in another.

The first Pentecostal meeting was held in 1906 in Norway, after Barratt returned from America. The meeting produced ecstatic manifestations and drew an enormous attendance. Many newspaper reporters from home and abroad visited Barratt's meetings in Norway. Prior to Pentecostalism in Norway, the Methodist Church was the largest Church outside the State Church. Later, Barratt was forced to resign from the Methodist Conference.

It was not Barratt's intention to leave the Methodist Church. He still had Methodist views of baptism during the first decade of Pentecostalism in Scandinavia. In 1916, he felt that it was necessary to organize the Pentecostals as an independent Church. After twenty years of Pentecostal life, Barratt held that it was not possible for a true Pentecostal believer to belong to any other church body.

In 1930, Norway had about 8000 Pentecostal believers. The expansion was very rapid; Block-Hoell (1964:23) points out that "In 1927-33, an average of more than one Pentecostal congregation was organized each month in Norway." In Oslo there were already four Pentecostal churches in 1933.

There were many church growth lessons to be learned:
1) Sensational press reports of the Pentecostal meetings greatly contributed to the success of the work.
2) The new converts had a truly a great missionary vision. They immediately went to other countries in Scandinavia, as well as Germany.
3) Barratt had literature in several languages. His articles were widely read in Scandinavia. Through his magazine, Korsets Seier, he kept contact with the various Pentecostal groups in the northern countries.

The greatest growth of the Pentecostals in Norway was in the period of 1930-1950. In 1950, they had about 30,000 members; in 1960, 35,000 members and 300 churches.

Sweden

The prophet of the Pentecostal Movement in Sweden was a Baptist minister, Lewi Pethrus. He and many other Swedish ministers had visited the Pentecostal meetings in Norway. Pethrus was baptized by the Spirit while in Norway and returned to his Baptist church in Stockholm that later changed into a Pentecostal Church. In 1913 he was excluded from the Baptist connection. The soil was well prepared for the Pentecostal revival. The low State Church revival had already cooled and people were longing for a new touch from God. The new revival was welcomed with joy, although it had exhibited ecstatic forms from the beginning.

Although the Baptists held that the reason for excluding Lewi Pethrus was his view of an open communion, the fact was that they were against Pentecostalism as an unsound movement. This exclusion was sensational in nature, and crowds of Pentecostally inspired believers left the Baptist connection. When Lewi Pethrus was called to be a pastor of the Filadelfia congregation in Stockholm, it had 29 members; at the present time its membership is 6,500. This church is the largest Pentecostal congregation in the world; it is the largest free church congregation in Scandinavia, having the largest religious meeting hall in Sweden, as well as a very considerable social work.

Since the Pentecostal movements are independent in all Scandinavian countries and are not organized into a union, no exact statistics are available. The Pentecostal movement in Sweden, however, is the largest in Scandinavia, having about 90,000 members and 560 churches at the present time   (Svanell, 1970).

The Pentecostal movement has not been spared separations. The first signs of these were prior to World War II. Sven Lidman, a Swedish author, had joined the movement in 1917, and soon became a strong figure there. His views differed from those of Pethrus, and they were both strong leading personalities. The schism resulted in the exclusion of Sven Lidman. In 1923 A. P. Franklin joined the Pentecostal movement and wanted to change its structure so that it would be more church-like. Franklin was a talented mission writer, but was excluded from the Pentecostal movement in 1929 in an unhappy controversy.

The most recent separation was in 1962, when Arne Imsen, a pastor in the Pethrus Pentecostal movement, withdrew with some followers to form a new Maranata movement. This has grown rapidly with the help of sensational reports. Most of the adherents come from the existing Pentecostal movement. The Maranata friends blame Pethrus for backsliding and engaging in non-essential things in the Pentecostal movement, such as politics and education, etc.

Without a doubt, Lewi Pethrus is the most outstanding free church leader in Scandinavia. His faith and vision have inspired thousands in Northern Europe.

We note certain lessons in church growth:

1) The Pentecostals have concentrated their work in most responsive areas: in North Götaland and in South Lappland in Sweden. In some of these areas the Pentecostals represent four per-cent of the population, and in other areas as much as ten, and up to thirty-nine percent (Nyhlen 1964:197).

2) The movement has had "inspiring and able leadership in the decisive decades." (Block-Hoell, 1964:91).

3) The Pentecostal movement has met a definite need in Scandinavia. It has offered liberty from the State Church structure, and given opportunity for praise and adoration by its members. The other existing denominations have had a more pessimistic version of Christianity to offer.

4) The subjective nature of Pentecostalism has found a good soil in the individual Scandinavians.

Denmark

Some clergy from Denmark visited Barratt's meetings in Norway in 1907. Returning to Denmark, they spoke favorably of the Pentecostals and invited Barratt to come to their country. The new revival movement did not shake Denmark in the same way as in Norway or in Sweden. The Press did not pay much attention, either, to what was going on in the religious world. This was also true of the preceding awakenings in Denmark in 1905.

Two famous actresses were converted at the height of their careers in 1908, and then became leading figures in the movement. During the first decade of Pentecostalism in Denmark, Barratt made several evangelistic trips there. Block-Hoell (1964:78) states that "to a greater extent more than in any other country, the interdenominational ideas of the early Pentecostal movement were practised in these first years in Denmark."

The organized Pentecostal movement is much smaller in Denmark than in all the Scandinavian countries. Block-Hoell (1964:74) believes that the reason for the slow growth in Denmark is that only small groups joined rather than churches, as was the case in other countries. The present membership is about 4,000.

Finland

A Norwegian Salvation Army Officer, G. O. Smidt, who had been in America and had joined the Pentecostals there, took the new movement to Finland. Some Finnish preachers had been in Norway and had heard Barratt. An invitation was extended to him, the Laestadians being the most eager to get Barratt to Finland. Preparation for this movement was done by literature. Ecstasy was not new; the Laestadians in the State Church expressed themselves in the same way as the Pentecostals did.

T. B. Barratt's first visit to Finland was in 1911, but no organized movement was established. Probably Barratt's alliance views were the reason for this. Barratt sent Smidt to Finland to continue the work, but unfortunately the American ways he had taken on were offending to the Finns, and after a while, even the most eager followers left him. Smidt's contribution to the Pentecostal movement in Finland was to introduce adult baptism and organize congregations to the movement.

In 1923, a split in the Pentecostal movement in Finland separated it into two camps: the congregational and the Pentecostal friends who wanted no part of organization. The latest estimate of membership of the Pentecostal friends is 3,600. The congregational group has about 30,000 members. The newest group, Finland's Free Mission, which compares with the Maranata friends in other Scandinavian countries, has about 1500 members. (Antturi, 1970).

The Salvation Army

As a result of the awakening in England in 1859, the Salvation Army was born. J. Edwin Orr points out that it was the "most significant and the most fascinating" (1965:169) development of the revival in the 1860s in Britain. The awakening also developed a social conscience among William Booth's followers, who followed doctrinally in the steps of John Wesley. The Salvation Army was the only denomination which grew out of the 1859 awakening in England. Misunderstanding from other denominations forced William Booth to

start a denomination of his own to exercise his double ministry of evangelism and social uplift. Years later, the awakening still had its effect. The rapid expansion of the movement
in the Scandinavian countries witnesses to this.

Sweden. (Frälsningsarmen)

Bramwell Booth, the mission general, had expressed an
interest to "open fire" in Sweden. He recognized the formal
Christianity in Sweden, but said: "there exists very little vital godliness " (Sandall 1950,II:284). The spiritual poverty in
Scandinavia was the justification of the Salvation Army's entrance to Lutheran, but nominal Christian countries. A Swedish woman, Hanna Ouchterlony, while visiting England, was
commanded by the General to begin a work. Before sending
the group of Swedes to their own country with the mission,
the General addressed them as "brothers and sisters." Upon
her return to Sweden, Hanna Ouchterlony reversed the order,
which read in the posters: "women and men speak and sing
about Jesus." (SAYB, 1968:12). The effect was that the meeting halls were fully packed in the first meetings in Stockholm in 1882. Arrests and riots were common in Sweden,
due to official and popular opposition.

The authorities tried by every means to quench the fire of
the new movement. Its leaders, mostly women, were taken
to prison. People of the community did not want to rent
their buildings to the Army for fear of reprisals. In the cold
Scandinavian winter, meetings were out in the open air. The
platform was made out of boxes turned upside down. The
Salvation Army historian, Robert Sandall, reports that the
people in those meetings numbered 5,000 (1950:285). In 1884,
only two years after the official entrance of the Salvation
Army to Sweden, 20,000 people crowded to hear the message
of the "Hallelujah Girls." "Everywhere, side by side, all
classes were found kneeling together at the penitent forms."

General Wickberg, the Swedish general, relates: "Sensational outward characteristics of the new movement--women
preaching, lively singing, brass bands, the flag, marching and
the preaching of holiness contributed substantially to the
early success of the Army in Sweden " (SAYB 1968:10).

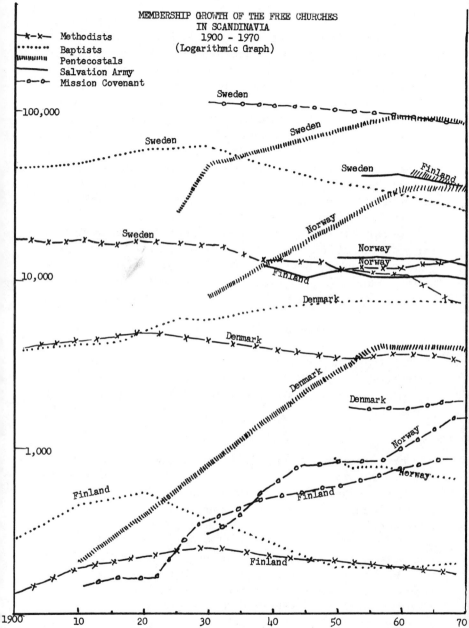

Figure 2

MEMBERSHIP GROWTH OF THE FREE CHURCHES
IN SCANDINAVIA
1900 - 1970
(Logarithmic Graph)

The first crisis in the Salvation Army in Sweden occurred in 1903, when five leading Army officers wrote to Bramwell Booth, asking for more democracy in the movement. They were patriotic Swedes and wanted an independent national leadership and use of their own funds and property by the Salvation Army in Sweden. Most important, however, was their appeal that the Army would follow the Swedish "Readers" type of Christianity. The General did not see any reason to change the principles laid down in England. In 1905, some of the patriotic officers were dismissed. Kaleb Svensson-Tollin became the leader of the Swedish National Salvation Army. It resembled the international Army, except in the partaking of sacraments (Nyhlen 1964: 220-222).

The Salvation Army in Sweden reached its peak in growth early in the 1960s. Then it lost about an average of 1,000 members a year, having a total today of 36,721 members (soldiers and officers). Figure 2 shows that the free church-constituency in Sweden as a whole began to decline.

Denmark (Frelsens Hær)

The Danes were next to accept the modern "Jesuits" to their country, in 1887. As other Danish free churches, the Salvation Army is small in membership, under 4,000.

Norway (Frelsesarmeen)

Commissioners Hanna Ouchterlony and Railton "opened fire" in Norway 1888. Norway was still united with the Swedish kingdom. Since the Norwegian and Swedish language were so similar, Hanna Ouchterlony, the Swede, became the leading officer and pioneer in that country. She adjusted herself easily to the familiar frankness and outspokenness of the Norwegians, and kept out of politics while there were tensions between the two countries. God blessed this courageous woman commissioner and during the first six months of their work in Kristiania, 4,000 seekers after salvation were reported (SAYB 1968:16). The young movement was not spared from crises. The first along this line came, when the English officers failed to recognize the individualistic

Scandinavian culture, and the rights of women in society. The British officers ignored the General-appointed women in authority in Norway. This caused Ouchterlony to write the General: "Norway has suffered" (1968:17). The General administered discipline. Another crisis developed with the emphasis on holiness. The very word "holiness" in the Scandinavian language does not convey the same meaning as the English word, thus creating much misunderstanding and confusion. In the 1890s this was a burning issue in the Salvation Army in Norway.

Today, the Salvation Army is declining in Norway, yet not as rapidly as in Sweden. The "Frelsesarmeen" is still the second largest movement in Scandinavia, Sweden being the first, in Salvationist organization.

Finland. (Pelastusarmeija-Frälsningsarmen)

The Army, which had its birth among common people and which was joined by people from the slums, began among the nobility in Finland. The first writings about the Salvation Army occurred un 1883 in the daily newspapers. (Könönen 1964:27) The official "opening fire" was in 1889. The pioneer trio made up of Louise af Forselles, Hedvig von Haartman and Constantin Boije (1964:33). Forselles was introduced to the Salvation Army through relatives in Switzerland. Later on she personally thought of the General as next to God. To the question: "Would the Salvation Army fit in Finland?" Forselles answered the General, "No, it is too noisy " (1964:42). However, Forselles then stayed for the officers' prayer-meeting. The presence of the Holy Spirit was strongly felt. Then Forselles gave a positive answer.

The first meetings held in Helsinki were in the Swedish language. It was a sensational occasion for Finland. Newspapers covered the story of the new army. To the first Salvation Army meetings came people from all classes in society. The meeting-hall proved too small (Könönen, 1964:53).

Prior to World War I, most of the present seventy corps were established. After the war, social institutions were established. Figure 2 illustrates the plateauing of the membership. Today there are 10,700 Salvationists in Finland.

PART II

What Can

Evangelical Missions

Offer?

5

Missionary—National Communication

That people should be treated as equals is commonly understood everywhere. This applies of course to communications between missionaries and European nationals.

In missionary-national relations, theory becomes practice. This relationship is also the most crucial level of communication. It tends to create many unnecessary tensions and misunderstandings, and hinders the growth of the church. Naturally, these tensions are more keenly felt in a small group than in a community of several thousands of members.

Both nationals and missionaries are strongly bound by culture. The problem is that it has been difficult for both parties to distinguish clearly which is really Christian and which is cultural tradition.

Many of the tensions which arise are rooted in the attitudes of missionaries and mission boards. Missionaries have been sent to Europe without anthropological training. To most missionaries, only one approach is needed. "My parents or grandparents came from the old country, I know the culture." Going to Europe to minister to the spiritual needs of the people with this attitude brings unpleasant surprises.

In mission work, it is always easier to learn a new language than to learn a new culture. We are accustomed to consider ourselves a integrated people on the basis of education, civilization, etc. However, this is not true. There are barriers in cross-cultural communication.

The Europeans tend to evaluate the American missionaries in terms of their own culture and vice versa. A visiting evangelist from abroad, faithful to the customs of his own country, changes his suit for each meeting. The nationals recognise this quickly; and for some nationals this is their very first acquaintance with a certain church. When asked what they thought of the revival, they answer; "I thought this was a church, and not a fashion show."

The nationals have a strong impression that Americans are "fancy." Thus, they are very seldom relaxed in the presence of the missionaries. They are concerned that their hospitality does not measure up to the level of the missionaries. Simply said, the nationals are afraid that they cannot be "fancy" enough for the missionaries to be accepted. This should not be interpreted as unfriendliness. It is rather the feeling that anyone has towards his superiors. The Hollywood style of Christianity has become a stumbling block.

Inter-Personal Relationships

The growth of the church suffers when there are tensions and bad relationships between missionaries and the nationals. Energy that was meant for building the church and winning lost souls is spent in strife. It seems to take extraordinary grace for both parties to come face-to-face in these matters.

A missionary preaching to the nationals that they should endure poverty for Jesus' sake, while he has a fine car and good salary, does not make sense. The Scandinavians often hold two jobs to improve their way of living. This is one way a person can climb up to the middle-class society and thus not be in the minority. This does not seem the right thing to do according to the missionary; although, with the two jobs, a national can only reach the missionary's level. Now and again the missionary tells the national of the sacrifice he made to come to Europe. In America, he received double the salary in the pastorate compared to what he gets now. This only increases jealousy. Riches have become a barrier to the people finding Jesus. Other sins of missionaries can be forgiven, but their wealth becomes such a hindrance in the minds of the less wealthy nationals.

The idea that the nationals are not aware of the weaknesses of the missionary is wrong. It is easy for the missionary to identify his own life with his message and to think that he is a nice perfect example to mankind. The problem arises, however, when the missionary does not want to admit his shortcomings. He continues in blindness, wearing a mask.

On the basis of inter-personal relationship, the foreign-sent church will stand or fall. The key to successful church growth is good communications. This should be considered seriously by the mission boards. By rectifying these matters sometimes in the national's favor, there would be a great leap forward towards church growth.

A missionary should have less voice in internal matters. The cooperation in the future depends on the policies the "mother" church practises today. W. Howard Conrad, a Nazarene missionary, presents the complaints of the nationals in his thesis. These complaints are still to be heard. Although they are from the Church of the Nazarene, they very well express complaints of other nationals:

a) Missionaries are too dictatorial.

b) Missionaries spend money intended to help us, buying cars and building fine homes for themselves.

c) We are subject to discipline and censure by the missionaries. Why should they not be subject to us in the same way? They should be under the discipline of the district they serve.

d) We ought to have a voice in deciding which missionaries will serve us.

e) We should be allowed to help decide where a missionary will serve.

f) If we are really a part of the Church of the Nazarene, why are we not permitted a part in governmental assemblies—such as the General Assembly or the General Board?

g) There ought to be a requirement that the mission let us know what funds have come and for what purpose they have been sent.

h) The Manual has been forced on us. If we have to live by it, why can we not have some voice in what is in it?

i) Why do so many missionaries insult us by not trying to learn our language properly?

j) Outside of business, missionaries have nothing to do with us (Conrad, 1967:465).

The younger church needs a missionary who is a true

friend, a partner in church planting, rather than a superior who dictates his will to the inferiors. The greatest is the one who serves. This is just as true on the mission field.

Brotherhood between the nationals and missionaries has received very little attention. When the missionary chooses friends on the field, they will more than likely be his equals —the other missionaries. The 'big shots' visiting from abroad tend to prefer fellowhip with the missionaries.

One way out of these problems is to develop a church with sound growth patterns. When the most important vision of the church or mission is to plant churches, troubles between nationals and missionaries will not become major problems. When there are many missionaries in a big church, relationships tend to be more healthy than in a little church.

Nida (1960: 216) suggests two principles for personal relationships. The first is equity and the other is love. The forms of equity vary in different countries. For the willing missionary, there are always some ways of equity upon the indigenous level.

The Missionary as a Leader

The leadership abilities of the missionary are important for good communication. An ordained minister at home in America may not necessarily have the knowledge of missionary administration. A pastor suddenly becomes the "big man" when going to Europe as a missionary. Success in administration has become the status symbol. A man is praised more for his accomplishments in real estate than in church planting. Buildings make more news in the mission magazines, than people who have found the Lord.

Some churches and missions in Europe have their own training institutes and Bible Schools to protect their doctrine. Naturally, young people are encouraged to attend these schools, although there might be some closer and less expensive for the student. The missionary leader does not consider that the Bible School trained young person may find some difficulties in the future if the church or mission does not make use of his services. The education received in a foreign-based institution may be counted against him.

Credit should be given for the kind thought prompting this provision to get the Europeans educated. It is important that the nationals reach the same educational level as their American colleagues. However, a few problems will arise when the national will decide to go all the way, and receive education beyond that of the missionary. Somewhere the missionary and the national have by-passed each other in communicating. The result is that the national with a higher education than the missionary will not be generally received with open arms in the company of his fellow workers.

The Missionary Drop-Outs

The short term missionaries have damaged church growth. This has resulted in the nationals not taking the new missionaries seriously any more. "They are not going to stay long anyway." "After they have satisfied their desire for sightseeing, they will go back to America." So the nationals are not always convinced of the missionaries' desire to be partners with them in church planting.

The Europeans also have some difficulties in understanding why, in cases of illness, the missionary must return to his home country. Europe is a civilized continent and has excellent hospitals. This kind of drop-out gives the impression that Europe compares with the African jungles. The sick missionaries will be shipped home from there if there are inadequacies in the medical field. Because of this and in other things, the superiority of the missionary increases.

The most serious drop-outs are those who become discouraged. The Europeans are accused of not being friendly enough. The people do not come to church in great numbers as they do in America. They do not get converted as easily as they do in America. The missionary gets discouraged. Finally he decides to leave. The whole thing is a question mark in the minds of the nationals.

The Missionaries' 'Yes-Men'

Not only the missionaries create problems, but so do the nationals. These are called the missionary's "yes-men."

They live to please the missionaries. No one becomes a "yes-man" voluntarily without direct or indirect encouragement. There is a selfish motive behind it. W. Howard Conrad (1967: 385), an experienced missionary, testifies:

> The weak "yes-men" so popular with missionaries
> will never push an aggressive program of self-propagation. Their every move is largely motivated by ideas
> of personal gain, and not by any vision of the Kingdom.

The "yes-men" are recognized by their "daddy, give me a banana" attitudes. They look upon the missionaries, the foreign-sent church or mission, as the "American Aunt or Uncle." Some Europeans have distant relatives in America. Occasionally they will visit their European relatives. When they come, they have "goodies" with them. One has to show his best side when the American Uncle is present, otherwise "goodies" will not appear. Rather than making some effort to raise money for their projects from their own people, they have special prayer for the "American Uncle" to come to the rescue.

The "yes-men" encourage a lazy ministry. It operates only when the missionary wishes. With an eye to the dollar, the "yes-men" are willing to be dictated to by the missionary. Often the missionaries talk about others who are "not willing to pay the price." To keep the church "pure," the national leaders with indigenous thinking and effort are pushed away. The mission boards should recognize this.

In the missionary-national relationships there are not any ready-made solutions, but we have guide lines to follow. The past mistakes should be avoided. If we can but learn from our mistakes, then God would bless our efforts for the Kingdom to a much greater degree.

Present Influence of Evangelical Missions in
Scandinavia
The Structures of the Mission Agencies

Dr. Ralph D. Winter discusses the different structures in the Winter 1969 issue of Evangelical Missions Quarterly, in the article "The Anatomy of the Christian Mission." He introduces the terms, 'vertical structures' and 'horizontal structures.'

A given Church which gets its financial support and personnel from within its own denomination is structurally called 'vertical' at home. When overseas, the Church continues in the same structure as at home; it is then called 'vertical-vertical.' The Church of the Nazarene is an example of this in Scandinavia. The interdenominational or the faith missions are 'horizontal' at home. They reach across many denominations to get their personnel and money. In their service overseas, they either continue in the same structure as at home, just being a "service mission" 'horizontal-horizontal' structure; or they can plant churches overseas, when we call them a 'horizontal-vertical' structure, as for instance, the Belgian Gospel Mission, which is a 'horizontal-vertical' agency.

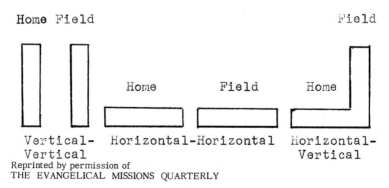

Home Field   Field

Home   Field   Home

Vertical-Vertical   Horizontal-Horizontal   Horizontal-Vertical

Figure 3

DIACHRONIC GRAPH OF THE ENTRY OF THE FOREIGN MISSION
AGENCIES IN SCANDINAVIA
1946-1968

YEAR	DENMARK	FINLAND	NORWAY	SWEDEN
1946				CEF
1947	CEF			
1948				
1949				
1950			CEF	
1951				
1952				
1953				
1954				
1955				
1956				GEM
1957				
1958	N			BCU,N
1959				
1960	Nazarenes			
1961				
1962				
1963	AEFCOF			
1964				YFCI
1965				
1966		CEF	GMU	Nazarenes
1967		BCM	YFCI	BCM
1968		CCC		

Date of entrance unknown:

	WLC	WLC	WLC	
	UPC	SCA		

Sources: North American Protestant Ministries Overseas
Directory 1968, IX:27-30; Allen 1969.

Figure 4

COMPARATIVE TABLE OF THE MISSIONARIES AND NATIONALS IN THE
FOREIGN MISSION AGENCIES WORKING IN SCANDINAVIA 1966/1967

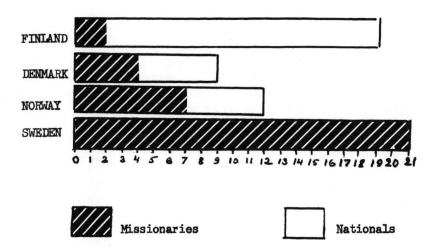

Sources: North American Protestant Ministries Overseas
Directory 1968, IX:27-30;   Allen 1969.

When the Protestant Mission agencies began they were all horizontal structures. They were free enterprises within a denomination just as we have free enterprises within the state. In a sense, we can call them Protestant orders, although they were without celibacy. The renewal movements in the State Church in Scandinavia are "orders." These horizontal structures which are copied from the Catholic Church, are more flexible than the vertical structure hierarchy in the Church. The horizontal structure has been their only means to do mission work. They have been able to take fast action. The Moravians were able to go to foreign missionary service at twenty-four hours notice. By the time the vertical structures have called a board meeting, the needy by Jericho's road have already died and been buried.

The horizontal agencies were born out of a deep need. In the Catholic Church before the Reformation, the horizontal structures (the orders) did the mission work. The hierarchy of the Church made missions difficult. New structures were needed. One of the reasons for the success in the Catholic Church is that it has been able to work in harmony with 600 orders within the Church (Winter, 1969:299). The Church has often taken the structural pattern of the society where it was born. The Roman Catholic Church took its structural pattern from that of the Roman Empire. Its dioceses were parallel to the geographical areas set up by the civil government. The roles of the priests were copied from the Roman civil magistrates. The theology or the purity of doctrine does not guarantee the success of any Church. The sects are often growing much faster than the "pure" churches. We are not so much concerned with the theology as with the structure, which makes the church mission either useful or useless.

The Church of the Nazarene

The Church of the Nazarene is, at present, the only church planting foreign mission agency in Scandinavia. The lack of spiritual vitality in Europe was the main reason Nazarenes felt it so necessary to enter Scandinavia. It was said by a Nazarene leader to be "one of the great challenges offered to the Church of the Nazarene today " (Johnson 1962:66). The "work" in Scandinavia opened in 1960. Copenhagen was the first city chosen for church planting, and five years later church planting efforts began in Stockholm.

Problems of Church Growth

The Nazarenes had a sincere compassion for the ungodly nations, and a burning desire to preach. Being Biblical in their proclamation, and conservative in theology, they certainly have a message to offer. Unfortunately proper plans for church planting were missing. From the church growth point of view, the following points would have needed special attention:

1) Romantic ideas were established before understanding the field, the peoples' customs and culture.

2) The attitude that after all, those who resist and hate the Christian message need mostly money and men has paralysed the Church. Ripe fields have not been considered priorities in strategy.

3) After ten years' work in Denmark, the Church of the Nazarene has thirty members, and after five years of labor only six members in Sweden. Since most of the "converts" are elderly people, the church does not have much possibility for expansion. In light of the great amount of foreign money given to the church in Scandinavia, the cost per "convert" has been extremely high. By recognizing the ripe fields and concentrating on them, the Church would have had better results, and the money sacrificially given would have been better used.

4) The stubbornness that seeing that we have come here, the Church of the Nazarene, we are going to stay, has limited vision and plans. The little Church with poor growth has been promoted at any cost.

5) The Church of the Nazarene has recognized the ripe fields for the Gospel in Norway and Finland (Johnson 1962) but although trained nationals have been available in both countries, no action has been taken for church planting there.

6) Thousands of dollars in foreign money have been invested in property, but the evangelistic program has been comparatively weak.

7) Lack of sufficient contact with other existing denominations and clergy in Scandinavia has given the public an impression of sectarianism.

8) The failure to win converts from the world has increased the unfriendly attitude of the other churches.

9) The structure of the church on the European field has been such that it has given very little freedom to the missionary or national to be "led by the Holy Spirit" in evangelism. The locations for evangelism have to be approved by higher powers which have very little knowledge of either the country or the people.

The Church of the Nazarene in Europe uses the right terms in church planting, like "indigenous Church." It has a sincere passion and excellent message, but unfortunately, the church planting has had little success.

Cultural Barriers

The greatest problem for church growth in the Church of the Nazarene in Scandinavia is that of the cultural barriers. Since the work is carried on by foreign missionaries, they can be identified with the nation only in a very limited way. At their best, they can become bilingual but not bicultural.

Usually in an ethnic group, change in culture is possible, but it goes on in a one-way direction. It is easier to move from a little minority group to a big majority. In Scandinavia it is easier for the free church members to return to the State Church than vice versa. Similarly, it is more likely that a Nazarene will go back to the traditional churches already established, than to be one of a minority group.

If a person identifies himself with a new minority group or a lower status, he soon comes under suspicion. This, it is felt, is unusual behavior. The general opinion in Scandinavia is that if anyone becomes a "fanatic believer" and joins the free church, he must be insane. A normal human being does not disown his own people in order to step down to isolation in a small group, where future opportunities are hazardous.

There is the danger that the free churches in Scandinavia stress membership too much, as this can separate the people from their fellowmen. Separateness on the ministerial and

Figure 5

DIVISION OF NORTH AMERICAN MISSIONARIES OVERSEAS

1966/1967

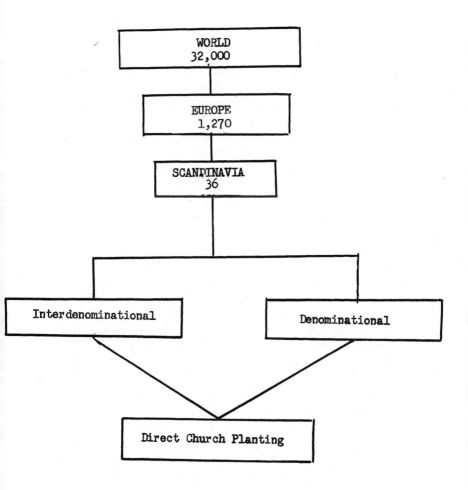

Sources: North American Protestant Ministries Overseas
Directory 1968; Allen 1969.

lay level destroy the possibilities of church growth. It positively brings certain closeness into the group. However, it hinders others from coming and joining when the group is too close. Visitors would feel like outsiders and less than cream of the group. This is more noticeable in a small congregation.

Interdenominational Missions in Scandinavia

Interdenominational mission agencies have also been called "service missions" or "faith missions," describing their purpose in aiding the existing denominations and their approach to the problem of personnel and financial support. They are non-denominational in the sense that they welcome workers and support from diverse sources. Lindsell (1962: 203) indicated that by 1962, about seventy-five per cent of all Protestant faith missionaries came from the United States.

The North American Protestant Ministries Overseas Directory (8th edition) indicates that more than 32,000 North American Protestant missionaries are serving overseas (1968: Section VIII, 2). From this group, 1,270 missionaries are serving in Europe. Breaking it down further, Scandinavia has only thirty-six missionaries, of whom only two are engaged in church planting, and even the church planting is declining. Europe has fifteen per cent of the world's population, but only two per cent of the North American missionaries serve there. Africa, which has more Christian influence than Europe has today, has more missionaries than Europe. Robert P. Evans, founder and European director of Greater Europe Mission, states that Europe is "an overlooked continent." (1963).

How effective are the "service missions"? The recent book, Latin American Church Growth, questions in general the effectiveness of the "service missions" from the church growth point of view. The "service missions" although having a greater amount of personnel and funds, have the poorest church growth results (Read, Monterroso, Johnson, 1969:58).

The "service mission" agencies working in Scandinavia have quietly fit into the picture among the existing denominations. The oldest of the foreign "service missions" in

Scandinavia is the Child Evangelism Fellowship. Its first missionaries came in 1946. Their work consists of conducting children's Bible classes usually in the homes, open-air evangelism, training courses for the teachers and translating literature to be used in child evangelism. The goal of CEF is to reach as many children as possible and bring them to a personal knowledge of Christ. The aid which CEF is providing for Scandinavia is needed, because of the poor Sunday School attendance. A hindrance to the work has been the general attitude of the existing denominations, especially the State Church's attitude——that conversion is not for children. The Finns made a Lutheran enterprise out of the CEF to avoid raising suspicions of the people. However, there is a work which is directed by the CEF International.

The facts based on the 1966 World Almanac indicate that in West Europe there are seventy three million children, and in Scandinavia close to seven million. There are thirty seven CEF missionaries working in Europe and nine of these serve in Scandinavia.

Child Population

Country	Population	Children
Denmark	4,702,904	1,567,635
Finland	4,603,000	1,534,333
Norway	3,704,000	1,234,666
Sweden	7,661,000	2,553,666
Total	20,670,904	6,890,300

The Greater Europe Mission, which entered Scandinavia in 1956, has ten missionaries working in Sweden. They are helping the existing denominations with evangelism and through a Bible Institute, which fills a real need in Sweden. The existing Bible Schools and Seminaries tend to be liberal and do not have sufficient place for Bible teaching in their curriculum. The new Bible Institute was enthusiastically received in Scandinavia evangelical circles in 1968.

The Bible Club Movement entered Scandinavia in 1966. In Finland they visited about seventy-five percent of all the high schools. In two years time 160,000 young people were

contacted from which 2,500 responded to the Bible Study program and follow up. Moody Science films are shown and the
students receive a Gospel of John each. The work in Finland
is now carried on by nationals. In Sweden, where the general attitude towards religion is cooler, the results have not
been as encouraging as in Finland.

In the Scandinavian countries, Campus Crusade for Christ
has been active in Finland only. A national worker has directed their activities since 1968. The purpose of CCC is mainly
person-to-person evangelism, evangelization through dis-
cussion groups and meetings on campus. The recent turmoil
in the universities in Finland, with propaganda literature
from Russia and China, has turned many young hopefuls for
the nation toward communism. Finland has universities in
seven locations, where over 60,000 students are enrolled.
Radio, press, and television have given a good coverage of
the Forerunners' concerts, which were attended by 14,000
students. CCC fills an important place in the student world,
challenging them for the new revolution.

Youth for Christ International has twenty-two missionaries in Europe and four of them are in Scandinavia. They are
active in Sweden and Norway. Their means of evangelization
are the youth camps.

The Bible Christian Union has a ministry in Scandinavia
to the Jews and children. They train laity for evangelism,
have camps for young people, and supply Christian literature.
Three of its twelve missionaries in Europe serve Scandinavia. The work in Finland is carried on by a national.

The Navigators concentrate on military bases, college
campuses and among the lay people. They organize Bible
Study groups and do person-to-person evangelism. Six of
their forty-three missionaries serve in Denmark, Norway
and Sweden. The Navigators' aid is valued because there is
a lack of good conservative Bible instruction in the existing
churches. Their goal is to produce mature Christ centered
Christians to share Christ with others.

The World Literature Crusade is supplying literature to
Denmark, Norway and Finland. All workers are nationals.
In Scandinavia eighteen national workers are engaged in
literature distribution, forty-nine outside Scandinavia in

free Europe.

The Church of Evangelical Fellowship and the United Pentecostal Church are raising funds to support existing Christian work. The America-European Fellowship for Christian Oneness does not have any personnel living in Scandinavia. An informant says that the work consists of personal soul-winning.

The horizontal structures, "service missions" would make a greater impact in Scandinavia, if they would allow the vertical structures to examine them. The secretiveness of the horizontal agencies makes people suspicious. The public does not know where the money, given to them, is going, and what, in fact, has been done. The public needs definite facts about the accomplishments of the horizontal structures. Only by honesty and openness can an effective cooperation be possible.

7

Can Evangelical Missions in Scandinavia Be Justified?

The Lutheran State Churches in Scandinavia are established by law and are controlled by the civil government. The new missions and movements have been accused of splitting the unity of the religious world. The existing denominations think they are the only ones who have the right to be in Scandinavia. How can new missions and denominations be justified? We might as well ask how Swedish Volvos in America can be justified? The United States has over half of all the world's automobiles. In the Western world, we believe in free enterprise. If there were not a need that the existing denomination could handle satisfactorily, there would not be a need for missions. We have already examined the accomplishments of the movements within the State Church and the free church denominations. Our study shows that only one of these denominations is growing at present in Scandinavia. The best rate of growth is in Norway. In Finland, the growth merely keeps up with natural growth. The other denominations are declining. Since the State Church growth is difficult to determine, we shall examine its effectiveness by church attendance.

Sweden

The most desperate problem in the Northern European countries is church attendance. The IRM states that never in the history of Sweden, except possibly during the first Christian centuries, has there been such a "building boom of parish houses and new churches as during the last few decades" (Vol. 53, 1964: 58) The large cities have become a mission field comparable to other traditional mission fields. Haland in his study, Väst Svenska Kyrka (1963) related that when people in the suburbs of Stockholm were interviewed, "sixty percent of the church members could not name a single minister in the Church" (1963: 198)

The age group, twenty-five to thirty-four, is the least represented in the church. Old people are in the majority in the church, and among these are more women than men. Age groups, ten to nineteen years; sixty to sixty-nine; and some over seventy, are overwhelmingly active attending church (Haland,1963:137,142).Some reasons for not attending church were given in a questionnaire:

a) We have too many organizations outside of the church.
b) We wish you to understand that we have different areas of interest: the pastor has the church, I have sports.
c) A laborer already belongs to too many groups, and does not have time to come to church (1963: 194).

The laborers, especially, felt that the Sunday service was too much for them. Sunday was the day to catch up with the work at home. Many who replied just wanted to rest from their heavy labor, on Sunday. Sunday was also one day when they could be at home. Young couples could not attend because of small children. The laborers held strongly that religion is a means to keep the laboring-class under the domination of the higher classes. Most disturbing of all is that several people felt they got very little or nothing out of the sermon or service (1963:180). The so-called intellectual said that the sermons were not relevant. They were too impersonal and did not have any human connection.

When asked what they did appreciate especially in the Swedish Church, the intellectual felt that it was good that the State Church was not emotional. The laborers appreciated most the fact that finally they have received the right to take their membership out of the Church (1963:185).It is the farmers, in Swedish society, who appear to be the most faithful to the Church. After their first Communion, the farmers are the most consistent in taking Holy Communion. The intellectuals are next and the laborers have the lowest attendance rate at Communion (1963:184). The laboring class also has the least confidence in the Church and its ministers. Most of those who rejected the privilege of speaking with a minister about personal matters, were laborers (1963:185). The majority of those interviewed missed warmth towards humanity in the Church. The laborers felt that the ministers are unable to live with the common people.

Church Attendance in Sweden

The percentage of males and females of those who attend church are as follows:

	State Church	Free Church	Population
Males	43	41	49
Females	57	59	51
Totals	100%	100%	100%

According to Halland's findings, the women are more likely to attend church, and they outnumber the men even more in the Free Church than the State Church. In 1969, the church attendance in Sweden was 2.4 percent of the population (Svenska Kyrkans årsbok, 1970).

Finland

An excellent study of the religiosity of the Finnish people and especially of the religious activity of those living in Helsinki, has been done by a sociologist, Koskelainen (1968). In the capital city, eighty-four percent of the population is Lutheran. The study was conducted in 1964 on a given Sunday in Helsinki. Out of those who attended church, 50.7 per cent went to the Lutheran State Church, and 49.3 percent attended the free church. During the divine service, only 32 per cent of the space available in the State Church was in use! At the evening vespers, 13 percent of the space available was in use (1968:11-12). The free churches had 44 per cent of their available space in use during the usual morning Sunday service. It is interesting to note in Finland, that good speakers draw people to a certain church. People who are hungry to hear the Gospel choose the church because of the speaker. During a normal Sunday, the church attendance in Helsinki was 4.7 per cent in 1964. At the same time, church attendance in other Finnish cities was: Tampere 6.1 per cent, Hämeenlinna 6.8 percent (1968: 98, 102, 104).

Adventists in Helsinki had the highest attendance percentage wise in relation to the members. Next was a radical

Figure 8

THE EIGHT MOST VISITED FINNISH SPEAKING CHURCHES AND GROUPS
IN HELSINKI, NOVEMBER 1964.

DENOMINATION	MEMBERS	MORNING SERVICE ATTENDANCE	ATTENDANCE PERCENTAGE OF THE MEMBERS
Adventists	459	483	105.2
Siion Congregation (Pentecostal)	800	600	75.0
Jehovah's Witnesses	1,322	989	74.7
Roman Catholic Church	1,400	357	37.3
Mission Congregation (Pentecostal)	600	168	28.0
Salem Congregation (Pentecostal)	4,124	520	12.6
Orthodox Church (State Church)	8,002	315	3.9
Ev. Lutheran Church (State Church)	369,473	7,128	1.9

1. Koskelainen's research shows that in a given Sunday November 1964, the people in Helsinki had an opportunity to visit 113 different religious services: 49 arranged by the Ev.Lutheran State Church, 9 by various revival movements inside the Ev. Lutheran State Church and 55 by others.

2. In November 1964, 84% of the population in Helsinki were members of the Ev.Lutheran State Church.

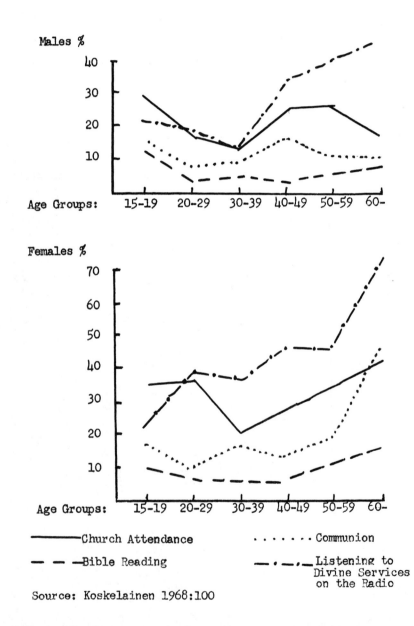

Figure 7

RELIGIOUS ACTIVITIES IN HELSINKI 1965.

Males and Females Belonging to Different Age Groups; Their
Church Attendance, Taking Communion, Listening to Divine
Services on the Radio and Their Bible Reading.

Males %

Age Groups: 15-19 20-29 30-39 40-49 50-59 60-

Females %

Age Groups: 15-19 20-29 30-39 40-49 50-59 60-

———Church Attendance   · · · · · · · Communion

— — —Bible Reading   —·—·—Listening to
                                    Divine Services
                                    on the Radio

Source: Koskelainen 1968:100

Pentecostal group that has been excluded from the main body. The Siion Congregation is followed by Jehovah's Witnesses and Roman Catholics in attendance. The Lutheran State Church is number eight in attendance, having 1.9 per cent of its members attending the divine services (1968: 10-11). Women over fifty years of age are the most active in attendance. The most passive are men in the age group of twenty to twenty-nine (1968:104). We must note that it is the same people who tend to attend church. Some occasional newcomers may be attracted to attend church at Christmas, which together with Advent Sunday, are most popular days for church attendance.

Since the common opinion in Scandinavia is that religion is shameful, there are many anonymous Christians who do not dare to express their needs which may well be spiritual needs. Religious matters are extremely embarrassing in Scandinavia. People do not want to take the risk that they may be recognized by some acquaintance if they went to church. Figure 7 shows that listening to divine service on the radio is most popular among both men and women, and the reason seems obvious.

Bible Reading and taking Holy Communion, which give an evidence of a deeper spiritual life, have been neglected by both men and women since their confirmation at the age of fifteen. After ten to fifteen years of age, other new interests arise. At the best and most meaningful period in their lives, the young people are missing the church and its message. The fact that the Church has not been able to reach the men is disturbing. The civil register, which mostly records those who do not want to be affiliated with any religious denomination, is dominated by men.

On the government-owned radio in Scandinavia, most of the radio and television services are censored. The message is watered down. Personal conversion is one of the neglected topics of the Church. The Marxist influence, in the labor class and among the intellectuals in the University campuses is reaping a harvest in Finland. Atheism and blasphemy have been much more open in society since the 1950s than ever before. This has been one of the reasons for decline in church attendance in Finland.

Figure 8

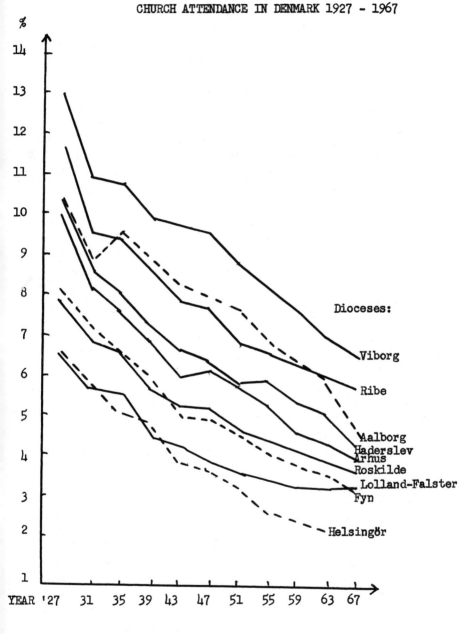

Figure 8

CHURCH ATTENDANCE IN DENMARK 1927 - 1967

Source: Andersen 1969:250

Denmark

Figure 8 illustrates the church attendance in Denmark from 1927 until 1967. According to the Danish Church Historical Society, average church attendance in Denmark was only 3.7 percent of the membership in 1967 (1969: 248-249). The church attendance varies in different parts of the country. It is lowest in the Copenhagen area, and Latourette mentions that in the 1950s only 2 percent of the population in Copenhagen attended the church regularly (1961, Vol. IV, 313). There is no reason to believe that the church attendance would be better today. In Denmark, as in other Scandinavian countries, more church buildings have been built than at anytime since the twelfth century. However, the churches in Copenhagen had only one seat to every seventeen of the population of the city; and in suburbs, only one seat for every thirty of the population (1961, Vol. IV, 313). During a regular Sunday, only a small proportion of the space available is in use.

Norway

The average attendance in Norway was 2.7 per cent of the population in 1957. The smaller parishes had greater attendances. The reason for this is the same as in other Scandinavian countries. The parishes are so large and the number of the clergy so small.

The average church attendance in Scandinavia is between 2.5 and 3 per cent as compared with the church attendance in the United States which is 50 per cent. If only 3 per cent of the population attend church in Scandinavia, then where are the 97 per cent of the population?

Lack of Workers

The ministry has become more and more unpopular in the Scandinavian countries. Many young men are leaving the ministry in Sweden. Never before has there been such psychological pressure upon the ministry. The modern theology evidently fails to give the courage to stand for Christ in an ungodly society. The Finnish Christian magazine, Uusi Tie, reports frequent cases of born-again Christians being fired from the State Church because of their concern for the salvation of others. Some of them have been sent to a psychiatrist, because their Christian life has differed so much from the dead nominalism. Every denomination reports a lack of workers. The best situation is in the Finnish State Church.

The official yearbook of the Lutheran State Church in Finland reports that, since 1938, more men are being ordained (SELK, 1968:68). However, this does not keep up with the population explosion. In 1966, the State Church had 1784 ministers and the number was expected to reach 2000 by 1970 (1968;69). The State Church has, in its service, 437 women theologians, and they expect an increase to bring this number to 700 by 1970 (1968:71). Finland is the only Protestant country in the world where there are so many theological students in proportion to the population. It has the largest number of women theologians, as well, who are full-time workers in the Church. The Bible Schools, Seminaries and Theological Faculties in Finland report the largest enrollment of all Scandinavian countries. This is one of the chief reasons why a foreign sent missionary's position cannot be too permanent in Finland. We have a sufficient number of well-trained workers in the State Church. The free churches are not so fortunate. The enrollment in their schools is declining, statistics show.

The three other countries, Norway, Denmark and Sweden, have not experienced much success in recruiting young people for the ministry. The quality of the ministry has become too professional. The clergy is involved in non-essential work most of the time. More churches have been closed than ever before. The ministry is not relevant and meaningful anymore. The clergy does not enjoy the same confidence from the public as in the previous decade. Disharmony between preaching and practising has caused bitterness in the public's reaction. The moral sins of the clergy have made front page news. As the people have witnessed so little sincerity in the ministers, they have lost their interest in the Church.

The Forgotten Minorities

The Scandinavian countries are almost homogeneous units, with the exception of the small minorities. According to Schwartz, Sweden has the greatest number of immigrants (1966). Sweden, as a welfare state, has been able to offer better living opportunities. Immigrants have come there to seek work. The Finns are the largest among the minority groups in Sweden. There are about 200,000 Finns in Sweden. The number of refugees and immigrants were:

Germans	50,000
Norwegians	40,000
Danes	35,000
Estonians	19,000
Jews	13,500
Hungarians	8,500
Dutch	8,500
Italians	8,500
Poles	7,000
Yugoslavs	7,000
Lithuanians	3,700
Czechoslovakians	3,500
Others	2,000

(1966:22)

Schwartz, who also is an immigrant, tells in his report, that the heavier and dirtier work is usually offered to the immigrants (1966:92). Their situation is much like that of the American Negro. They are not only forgotten physically but spiritually as well. . . Few of them are able to find their way into the church fellowship. The Lutheran Church has Finnish speaking services for the Finns in the major cities of Sweden. In Stockholm, for instance, the church attendance among the Finns in 1959 was 0.9 per cent of the membership of the Finnish Church. At the same time, church attendance in Helsinki was 2 per cent (Koiranen 1966:68,69). Koiranen, the sociologist who conducted the research among the Finns in Sweden, points out that their religiosity is not voluntary by choice, but that the Finns attended church because of their need for security in a foreign country (1966:70).

Denmark has the second largest group of immigrants and in 1950 records revealed that two per cent of their population was born outside the country.

Germans	25,320
Swedes	18,280
Norwegians	7,890
Americans	3,790

(Sachs 1963: 63)

The Lapps

There are very contradictory reports about the Lapps who live in Scandinavia. The most reliable is the sociological study by Erkki Asp, published by the Turku University (1965). He estimates the Lapps in Finland, Norway and Sweden to be at least 30,000 (1965: 18-19). There are also contradictory statements of who the Lapps are. A lack of knowledge of the Lapps has resulted in even the Government statistics giving contradictory information. The researchers in this area agree that there are today more Lapps living in Scandinavia than ever before (1965:19). They are found in each country:

Norway	(1952)	22,000
Sweden	(1945)	10,193
Finland	(1964)	3,176

(1965: 18, 240)

The growth of the Lapp population in Scandinavia is expected to be greater than it has been before. However, Lapps will continue to be a minority there. In Finland, 83 percent of the Lapps use the Lappish language as their mother-tongue. Asp's study indicates that the desire to keep the old traditions alive is found more among the older generation. The literature and radio programs were more popular when they were presented in the Lapp language, and they preferred to have more communications in their own language (1965: 242-243). Other suggestions made by Lapps in Finland were

1) Itinerating pastors for the churches.
2) More pastors who know Lappish.
3) Divine services in Lappish.

4) Churches should have interpreters who know Lappish.
5) Sunday Schools in Lappish should be organized.
6) Religious instruction in the public schools in Lappish.
7) Planting of new churches in Lappish neighborhoods.
8) More house meetings.
9) Church choir singing in Lappish.
10) Use of old Lappish marriage customs.
11) A more active youth program in the church.

(1965:226)

Asp's research shows that Christianity has influenced the change of the old traditions in the Lappish culture. The Laestadians, who are conservative and do not like change, are most widely spread in Lappland. They have preserved their old traditions and have a unifying effect upon society (1965: 200).

Since the Lutheran Church is the State Church in Scandinavia, they also have some churches in Lappland; and the Salvation Army has missionaries working in Swedish and Norwegian Lappland.

The Gypsies

Gypsies are estimated to have a population of about two million in the world. The first report of their appearance in Europe was heard from a Franciscan monk in 1322 (Vehmas 1961:32). Gypsies are found mainly in Sweden and Finland.

Finland	4,000
Sweden	8,400

(1961:41; Schwartz, 1966: 91)

The Gypsies have large families and they are a growing ethnic group today. They are constantly on the move, and those who are not Gypsies have a hatred of them.

Although the Gypsies are baptized as is the rest of the Scandinavian population, they have very little knowledge of Christianity. Their religion is primitive magic (1961:134) Although the Gypsies do not attend church faithfully, they are not resistant toward Christianity. They allow their children to be baptized in the State Church. Figure 9 illustrates

Figure 9

CHURCH ATTENDANCE OF THE GYPSIES IN FINLAND 1960

Church Attendance of the Rural and Urban Gypsies (%)

Time When Last Attended	Rural	Urban	Total
Less than one month ago	21	17	19
Less than one year ago	41	27	36
More than one year ago	21	20	24
Do not attend	13	30	21
Total	100	100	100

Church Attendance of the Male and Female Gypsies (%)

Time When Last Attended	Males	Females	Total
Less than one month ago	13	24	19
Less than one year ago	27	44	36
More than one year ago	31	13	21
Total	100	100	100

Source: Vehmas 1961:210

the religious activities of the Gypsies in Finland. They do not differ from the common pattern. The females are more religious and attend church more than the males do. Also, the rural Gypsies are more active in church attendance than the urban ones. The State Church in Finland has an organization called the Gypsy Mission. It expresses a social concern for the Gypsies mainly. The spiritual welfare of this ethnic group needs much consideration. The Gypsies are strongly clan-conscious. Vehmas' study indicates that 88 per cent did not belong to any organization of the "whites," as they call the Scandinavians (1961:211).

Though often neglected by the Christian Church, the minorities are dear to God. When oppressed in society, God has sent His servants to plead for forsaken peoples. God is concerned in their justice and spiritual welfare.

These minority ethnes in Scandinavia are receptive today. The Lapps have especially expressed their growing desire to worship God in their own language (Asp 1965:226). The Gypsies have their own language, which they prefer to use. In 1954, 71 per cent of the Gypsies spoke it (Vehmas 1961: 93). The attitude of the sixteenth century Church, expressed by Archbishop Laurentius Petri, is still alive today: "The priests must not communicate with the Gypsies, nor baptize their children, or bury them " (1961:47).

Just people make a just society. The signs of God's Kingdom are "the poor have good news preached to them " (Matt. 11:5). Christ was sent "to proclaim release to the captives and recovery of sight to the blind, to set at liberty those who are oppressed, to proclaim the acceptable year of the Lord " (Luke 4:18). The spiritually poor are close to God's compassionate heart.

The Potential Role

of Evangelical Missions

In this chapter, we shall present brief guidelines and re-
commendations and discuss plans for new mission agencies
to come to Scandinavia. A cold religious atmosphere, a declining church membership, a continually declining church
attendance, and the existence of evangelistically neglected
groups of people force us to conclude that Scandinavians
need foreign evangelical missions at this time.

Guidelines for Mission Agencies

Homogeneous Unit Churches. This term means a church
which is growing exclusively within a single segment of society. McGavran believes that homogeneous unit churches grow
more rapidly than those which try to unite several cultures.
When a church grows in a homogeneous unit, the goal must
result in winning the whole population of that segment. The
homogeneous units can be observed by noting the pattern of
how people marry in a society. A homogeneous unit is:
> a society whose members marry exclusively within
> it. Whether such a caste or tribe is really racially
> distinct from others is really immaterial. As long as
> its sons take wives only from the people itself, so
> long will it think of itself as a really separate race...
> (McGavran 1962: 5).

The homogeneous units share common characterestics, people consciousness which make them think as "one people."
Even in the so-called civilized societies, homogeneous units
can be seen (1965:71).

McGavran gives three principles about homogeneous unit
churches:
1) Each homogeneous-unit Church flourishes best under
   its own leaders.
2) Each denomination in each homogeneous unit of the
   general population needs its own church organization.

    3) Each homogeneous-unit church has its own measure of
       responsiveness to the Christian message (1965: 77ff).
    The church growth theory advocates that this is the day
of increasing receptivity. The harvest fields are white. God's
will for them is to find them. Nations as a whole seldom become responsive, but small segments of the society will.
McGavran points out:

> When people are turning responsive as social classes,
> as peasants moving into cities, as tribes, castes,
> tongues, and numerous other ethne, the biblical man-
> date to bring the ethne to faith and obedience falls on
> our ears with particular force. Not only is there the
> command, but God has provided the opportunity (1970:
> 63).

People do not become receptive by accident. God is Sovereign.
He makes the people willing to hear and to receive the Good
News. In the fullness of His time, God calls His people out.
Some of the causes for receptivity are:

    1) New Settlements. Immigrants are open for many kinds
of innovation. The Pentecostal growth in Brazil took place
mainly among the immigrants. Immigrants in new circumstances are insecure. They willingly accept refuge.

    2) Returned Travelers. The first free church pioneers
in Scandinavia became Christians while traveling abroad.
They returned to their countries and planted churches.

    3) Conquest Affects Responsiveness. During wars,
Scandinavia has been very responsive to the Gospel. People
have sought refuge in God. Finland and Norway, as the
Scandinavian countries most recently involved in war, are
even now more humble and tender towards the Christian
message.

    4) Nationalism. The Finns and the Norwegians are the
most patriotic people in Scandinavia. In Finland, revival
and nationalism went hand in hand during the great Pietist
revivals.

    5) Freedom from Control. Over one-third of the world
is under a strict system of control. This may hinder church
growth from being its fullest.

    The Indigenous Church. Any missionary agency should
understand and intelligently practise indigenous principles.

We must understand the difference between church growth theory and indigenous church theory. The former concerns itself with the fact of church planting, while the latter concerns itself with the kind of church to be planted. The indigenous church has as its formula--- a) self-support; b) self-government; and c) self-propagation.

The traditional method is for the mission to select some men from the converts to become pastors or evangelists who will be paid by the mission or the mother church. It is true that nationals are more capable in knowing their own language and culture. But this method presents some disadvantages. Some would like to join the church planting mission in order to get a job.

Self-support. Hodges (1953: 70-79) offers these eight arguments for self-support:

a)   It is biblical.

b)   It is logical.

c)   The spiritual welfare of the congregation demands it.

d)   The pastor needs to feel his responsibility to his congregation rather than to the mission.

e)   The faith and sacrifice of the workers develop a vital spiritual ministry.

f)   Without the mission's support, the worker learns more responsibilities.

g)   Self-support puts the national workers financially on the same level as his countrymen, with obvious benefits.

h)   Self support encourages expansion.

In a modern Scandinavian society, and especially in the highly resistant areas such as Sweden and Denmark, self-supporting principles should be practised, to avoid tying the mission's money up where there is no immediate harvest. In a nearby area, such as Finland and Norway, the harvest might be ready for harvesting, but is in danger of being spoiled because of unwise mission policies.

Self-government. By self-government we do not mean that the structural form of the church has been imported in a package deal from a foreign country. The church gets a government that way, but it is not indigenous. Smalley points out that that type of church is "... governed in a slavishly foreign manner" (Smalley 1958:52).

Self-propagation. Foreignness hinders self-propagation, but we must not think that any daughter church rising against the mother church would have a truly indigenous desire. The reasons for doing this must be examined. We wonder why indigenous churches grow better than others. McGavran gives these reasons:

a) A missionary following indigenous principles, primarily sets priority to church planting.

b) Non-Christians recognize the unpaid leaders, who are people like themselves in the indigenous church (McGavran, 1970: 340-343).

The Need for Church Planting Missions

The urban areas in Scandinavia provide the greatest challenge to any mission. The existing denominations have not found the ways of introducing Christ and bringing people into the fellowship of the Church. Three kinds of structural forms are possible in the Scandinavian countries.

1. Church Planting Service.

We need mission agencies, either horizontal or vertical structures, to plant churches in Scandinavia and then turn them over to the existing denominations. This type of church planting probably would be best received. There would not be so much suspicion of "sheep stealing." Since at the present, many churches do not have sufficient workers, and many of them do not have the vision or skills to plant churches, this kind of help in the urban areas would be welcomed. The national churches would get the full credit. The mission would render this service and then let the nationals carry on the work. For all church planting in the urban situation, churches in the home are recommended.

For the Scandinavian, the most natural setting to hear the Gospel is in the home. Scandinavians visit frequently in each other's homes and chat over a cup of coffee. In our study, we have already pointed out that the Scandinavians feel embarrassed to enter a local church. They could come to a private home without embarrassment. House churches have had and will have an important place in church planting in Scandinavia.

(a)   House churches are Biblical.   The Bible does not exhort anyone to worship in a special building. Oppressed Christians behind the Iron Curtain often so worship. It is not less spiritual to worship in a home.

(b)   As history shows, God has broken many traditions when He has desired to bless His people and claim to Himself the lost.   The Pietist revivals in Scandinavia began in homes.   When the existing churches had failed to meet their spiritual needs, people began a church in their homes where there was Bible study and prayers.   "Homeless Christians" in Scandinavia still gather in homes around the Word of God.

(c)   House churches are financially practicable. A small group of believers meeting in a large city would not be able to finance a church building.

(d)   Building new churches would be an unwise policy in today's Scandinavia, where the laboring class is bitter over the way the churches are using their money for monuments to the dead while failing to recognise the needs of the living.

(e)   The receptivity of the Gospel is greatest in the cities. People are moving there constantly.   They are more likely to adopt new ideas.

(f)   The established churches have the greatest opportunity to plant hundreds of daughter churches in the cities.

(g)   House churches can be planted also in the rural areas.

2. Planting a New Denomination

An example of the present denominational church planting foreign evangelical mission in Scandinavia is the Church of the Nazarene, which we have discussed earlier. Structurally, the most successful would be a denomination which would have its headquarters in the country served. Internationalism in the Church is good, but not the best from the church growth point of view.   Orders from foreign headquarters are not well received.   Another example is the Methodist Church which shows how bureaucracy has produced an ineffective organization in some foreign fields. Adjusting to the culture in which they serve should be considered for greater success.

3. An Independent Society of Believers in the State Church.

An example of this type of structure is the Evangelical Fosterlands Stiftelsen in Sweden. It is an independent organization within the State Church. It takes care of its own affairs and can freely evangelize without suffering pressure from any dominating organization. The Salvation Army, though following doctrinally the Wesleyan tradition, has its members and adherents recognized as members of the State Church in Scandinavia. In Sweden, most of the free church members are also members of the Church of Sweden.

Naturally, this is only a formality, which however does not hinder believers from exercising their faith and vision freely within their spiritual home. The State Church membership ensures a wider acceptance by the society. Since the State Church has become a symbol of patriotism in all of Scandinavia, a mission agency recognizing the loyalties of Scandinavians and not insisting that they leave the State Church which symbolizes that loyalty, could provide a spiritual home for them in an independent organization, and thus make the most of a great opportunity in church planting.

The Need for Service Missions

By service missions, we mean those agencies that would serve all denominations and not necessarily be involved in a direct church planting operation. The suggestion is made only if there is not already a parallel agency in Scandinavia. We have already noted that horizontal agencies have had poor records for church growth in Scandinavia. They should not be encouraged to come unless they have definite goals in evangelism and unless they meet a real need.

There is an obvious need for a Church Growth research agency. Reasons for growth and non-growth need to be made available to Churches, movements, mission agencies, pastors, missionaries and laymen. The average church member is not even aware that his church is declining. Circumstances are often blamed for poor growth, when the real reason is lack of church growth understanding, a skill which must be developed. This kind of agency, probably first of all run by missionaries with national assistants, could be operated by national staff as soon as these are trained. The importance of at least a formal national leadership in the beginning could not be over-emphasized, otherwise its mission might become misunderstood.

Annually, this agency should evaluate the results of the yearly efforts in various churches and organizations, and then publish them for close study by Christians in responsible positions. Facts help evaluation of faithfulness to God in the worldwide mission that He entrusted to His servants. If the agency operates sympathetically, it will make a great contribution to church growth in Scandinavia.

Seminary education by extension is another need. Since most of our training institutions tend to be liberal and have lost their vision and passion for evangelism and the importance of God's Word, foreign help is needed in this area. The Guatemala seminary program was first instituted by the Presbyterians and favors "on-the-job" training. Its philosophy is to go to the existing natural leaders in the society and train them where they labor rather than to bring them to a traditional three-year residential course in theology. Mature men and women in the society already carry heavy responsibilities; they are already motivated to learn; and they can support themselves and their families while they learn in the Extension program. Thus Extension education makes it possible for everyone to study. It is financially practicable now. The student is treated as an adult in his own society and culture. Many church evangelistic programs suffer because of the prior demands of a traditional school for a few students. Only the very privileged are usually selected for the traditional ministerial training. By looking for the brilliant young man to be the pastor, the church often walks by the real, mature leaders in the society. The Extension program would provide a valuable supplement to existing traditional ways of training.

Pentecostal growth in Brazil demonstrates how the New

Testament pattern for training the ministry has proved to be efficient. To Pentecostals, ministry which does not bear good fruit is not of God. If the candidate fails in this, he must step aside. Paid ministry in the traditional churches tempts those who are neither called of God nor have the gifts to qualify. The tent-making pattern of ministry provides greater room for the expansion of the church, and continues even if mission support fails or funds at home do not come in. And the growing church takes pride in its autonomy.

The Seminary Extension program operates on different levels: Bible School level, College level, and Seminary level. If it is a branch of a North American Theological Seminary, and would grant degrees to students in Europe, it would keep many promising young people in the Church in Scandinavia. Once in North America, the Scandinavian student finds the temptation too great to stay. Foreign church planting agencies do well to take this into consideration. Nationals sometimes want to have evangelistic training beyond the Bible college level without coming to the United States.

Ralph D. Winter's <u>Theological Education by Extension</u> gives further details of the operation of this kind of Seminary.

Missionary Recruiting Agency. Vast resources of warm-hearted, dedicated and skillful laymen are left unused for overseas service. Single people, both men and women and those over thirty years of age and childless couples, should not be left out of consideration for mission service overseas. These may be responsible, mature and capable. In many cases, they are able to pay their own way to the mission field for short-time service. Recognizing that in some cultures their social status could be a handicap, other cultures could be designated where they could be effective. The policy of some mission boards that everyone must be married to be a capable missionary is as poor an extreme as that in the Roman Catholic Church where the clergy must remain single. Christ recruited His missionaries from all categories. If such people were good enough for Christ, why not for His Church? With little flexibility, willingness and good management and missionary skills, hundreds of self-supporting personnel from the Scandinavian countries could be placed yearly in overseas service.

Audio-Visual Service Agency. A central organization for the Scandinavian countries is needed to provide audio-visual materials. In this area of service, the United States has much to offer. Evangelistic 8mm films could be used in the house churches, for 8mm movie projectors have become popular in home use. Tapes and casettes could be used in either evangelism or education. A Scandinavian would rather listen to the Gospel on tape in privacy than have somebody visit him in his home to convert him. The Extension Seminary program as well as existing churches, missions and their personnel could benefit much from this service.

The Need for Agencies Aiding in Evangelism

A special mission agency is needed to bring horizontal and vertical agencies together. Examples of this type of service are found in the Billy Graham Evangelistic Association and Evangelism-in-Depth. Evangelism is a most urgent need, which traditional Churches have failed to recognize. A united effort in evangelism by all Christians from all denominations provides a strong testimony to the world. Both these agencies mentioned have demonstrated that it is possible to bring Christians together in seeking the lost.

Many of the traditional Churches do not have evangelists, as such, for special meetings and, if they do, the evangelists are the first to be removed from their field if the money gets tight. Priorities in evangelism should be re-emphasized. Today, the majority of the Scandinavian population is under twenty-five years of age. Only a few of these are active in the Church. The suicide rate in Scandinavia is one of the highest in the world. Divorces and illegitimate births and crime have broken all records of the past. Never before have blasphemy and atheism been so openly exercised. The Counselor of the Court of Appeals in Finland, Paavo Hiltunen, said: "Only an old-fashioned, Holy Ghost revival can save our nation" (1970: 2). All Scandinavia needs revival.

In this study, we have surveyed the developments and formation of organizations to communicate the Good News, and evaluated them from the church growth point of view.

Church growth is a complicated phenomenon that depends upon many social and political factors as well as faithfulness to God in witness and method. It seems difficult to predict whether personal Christianity will survive in Scandinavia. The decline in the Churches alarms any concerned Christian. Segments of the society are more responsive than they have ever been before. Present resources in Scandinavia for successful church planting and multiplication of churches are better than they have ever been before. Scandinavians need no financial assistance; they need spiritual uplift.

Church planting evangelism must be greatly increased. We need the North Americans to demonstrate this to us. Most of the mission budget for Scandinavia should be used in direct evangelism. Theological training should produce men and women successful at church planting. Unpaid men should be ordained. Every convert mobilized for soul-winning. New offices created in the church so that all members of all classes, backgrounds and civil status have a place of service according to their calling and gifts.

Although we recognize the desperate hour, there is also hope. In the darkest times God has often chosen to revive His people and awake the sinners. Beyond all programs and human church growth skills we look to God for the outpouring of the Holy Spirit. The believers in Christ are tempted sometimes to cry with Habakkuk: "Oh Lord, how long shall I cry for help, and thou wilt not hear"? (Hab. 1:2) Being in despair, he heard God say: "For I will work a work in your days, which ye will not believe, though it be told you " (1:5).

> If my people which are called by my name, shall humble themselves, and pray, and seek my face, and turn from their wicked ways; then will I hear from heaven, and will forgive their sin, and will heal their land (II Chronicles 7: 14).

In Scandinavia, we stand in the midst of a valley of dead bones, spiritually speaking. The Prophet Ezekiel said, "They were very dry, And he said unto me, Son of man, can these bones live?" In the vision, the prophet saw a new life in them. "...and a breath came into them, and they lived, and stood up upon their feet, an exceeding great army " (Ezek. 37) Scandinavia needs uplift because its declining churches and spiritual laxity do not only affect Northern Europe but the whole world. When the churches at home are powerless, the missionary giving and personnel also decline, thus affecting the world picture of Christianity. Where are today's Pietists and Moravians, the champions of the 'heart' religion, with their eager missionary spirit? Could these missionaries with warmth and assurance of their faith be a tool to reach a new John Wesley in Europe? Will God give us new Hauges, new Ruotsalainens, and new Roseniuses for Scandinavia? Each Church, mission and Christian must seek guidance from God and pledge complete faithfulness to Him that the Church of Jesus Christ might grow and be strong so that "the gates of hell shall not prevail against it " (Matt. 16:18).

Appendices

APPENDIX I: STATISTICAL TABLES

A. STATISTICS OF A RELIGIOUS SURVEY IN HELSINKI
1965

This Table Shows When Church Was Last Attended According to Age and Sex in Helsinki
(In Percentage)

AGE GROUP	15 - 19		20 - 29		30 - 39		40 - 49		50 - 59		60 -	
M-males; F-females	M	F	M	F	M	F	M	F	M	F	M	F
Less than two months ago	29	34	17	36	12	19	24	27	25	33	16	43
Two months to eight monts ago	29	34	22	21	27	14	23	24	25	28	12	17
Eight months to and a half years ago	27	23	26	24	16	38	20	27	18	18	28	15
Over two years ago	15	9	35	19	45	29	33	29	32	21	44	25
TOTALS	100	100	100	100	100	100	100	100	100	100	100	100

STATISTICS OF A RELIGIOUS SURVEY IN HELSINKI
1965

This Table Shows When Communion Was Last Attended According to Age and Sex in Helsinki
(In Percentage)

AGE GROUP	15 – 19		20 – 29		30 – 39		40 – 49		50 – 59		60 –	
M-males; F-females	M	F	M	F	M	F	M	F	M	F	M	F
Less than two months ago	12	9	3	5	4	5	2	5	4	9	6	15
Two months to eight months ago	44	54	10	15	4	6	10	9	13	18	3	30
Two years and eight months to ten and a half years ago	26	17	59	60	6	14	4	19	12	13	13	16
Over ten and a half years ago	0	0	20	17	82	68	82	59	66	55	69	34
Never	18	20	8	3	4	7	2	8	5	5	9	5
TOTALS	100	100	100	100	100	100	100	100	100	100	100	100

STATISTICS OF A RELIGIOUS SURVEY IN HELSINKI
1965

This Table Shows When Divine Services Were Last Listened to Over the Radio in Helsinki (In Percentage)

AGE GROUP	15 – 19		20 – 29		30 – 39		40 – 49		50 – 59		60 –	
M-males; F-females	M	F	M	F	M	F	M	F	M	F	M	F
Less than one week ago	21	20	18	38	12	36	32	46	39	46	44	74
One week to two and a half years ago	32	26	44	40	53	45	39	36	34	36	40	14
Over two and a half years ago or never	47	54	38	22	35	19	29	18	27	18	16	12
TOTALS	100	100	100	100	100	100	100	100	100	100	100	100

STATISTICS OF A RELIGIOUS SURVEY IN HELSINKI
1965

This Table Shows When the Bible Was Read According to Age and Sex in Helsinki

(In Percentage)

AGE GROUP	15 – 19		20 – 29		30 – 39		40 – 49		50 – 59		60 –	
M-males; F-females	M	F	M	F	M	F	M	F	M	F	M	F
Less than two weeks ago	15	17	7	9	8	16	16	12	9	18	9	47
Two weeks to four months ago	29	14	17	21	27	17	21	20	18	28	19	22
Over four months ago	41	57	70	65	61	56	55	53	61	45	59	23
Never	15	12	6	5	4	11	8	15	12	9	13	8
TOTALS	100	100	100	100	100	100	100	100	100	100	100	100

B. FORTY YEARS OF CHURCH ATTENDANCE IN DENMARK

YEAR	CHURCH ATTENDANCE	POPULATION – CHURCH ATTENDANCE	POPULATION + CHURCH ATTENDANCE	TOTAL POPULATION	PERCENTAGE
Diocese: Fyn					
1927	19.635,7	236.731	10.559	341.290	8,30
1931	20.930,9	284.459	63.214	347.673	7,36
1935	17.740,5	261.109	86.429	347.538	6,79
1939	17.009,9	277.210	86.472	363.682	6,14
1943	15.557,2	297.379	67.122	364.501	5,23
1947	15.604,9	304.087	72.944	377.031	5,13
1951	15.032,3	317.604	62.504	380.108	4,73
1955	13.695,8	321.325	81.072	402.397	4,26
1959	12.867,2	327.735	77.132	404.867	3,93
1963	12.340,7	333.211	82.313	415.524	3,70
1967	10.357,1	313.994	112.268	426.262	3,30
Diocese: Hadesrslev					
1927	19.061,5	181.205	79.300	260.595	10,51
1931	17.405,9	196.528	68.507	265.035	8,86
1935	16.598,6	202.237	62.547	264.784	8,21
1939	15.565,3	210.765	65.946	276.715	7,39
1943	14.652,0	216.442	63.174	279.616	6,77
1947	15.316,7	233.903	65.699	299.602	6,55
1951	14.044,8	235.000	67.841	302.841	5,08
1955	11,770,3	195.625	121.386	317.011	6,02
1959	11.397,6	206.106	122.140	328.246	5,53
1963	11.528,0	201.137	123.621	342.758	5,26
1967	11.548,7	260.752	102.517	363.269	4,43
Diocese: Helsingør					
1927	9.266,6	135.400	135.441	270.850	6,84
1931	9.233,5	155.651	156.355	312.006	5,93
1935	8.384,3	158.793	190.701	349.584	5,28
1939	10.243,2	205.265	221.440	426.705	4,99
1943	9.868,5	244.850	244.438	489.288	4,03
1947	11.555,6	302.722	233.528	536.250	3,82
1951	9.548,2	278.178	283.901	562.079	3,43
1955	9.374,0	339.849	286.481	626.330	2,76
1959	9.569,4	380.189	334.594	714.783	2,52
1963	9.293,3	394.427	406.759	801.186	2,36
1967	10.075,2	473.486	409.966	883.452	2,13

YEAR	CHURCH ATTENDANCE	POPULATION - CHURCH ATTENDANCE	POPULATION + CHURCH ATTENDANCE	TOTAL POPULATION	PERCENTAGE

Diocese: Viborg

YEAR	CHURCH ATTENDANCE	POPULATION - CHURCH ATTENDANCE	POPULATION + CHURCH ATTENDANCE	TOTAL POPULATION	PERCENTAGE
1927	24.205,2	185.516	54.065	239.581	13,05
1931	22.485,4	205.162	42.603	247.765	10,96
1935	21.617,7	199.989	47.695	247.684	10,81
1943	22.490,4	228.446	30.137	258.583	9,84
1947	23.968,4	247.696	26.490	274.186	9,68
1951	21.932,4	247.399	27.996	275.395	8,87
1955	20.905,1	252.343	33.066	285.409	8,28
1959	21.111,1	272.213	27.600	299.813	7,76
1963	20.737,3	294.066	11.664	305.730	7,09
1967	20,455,0	307.607	13.968	321.575	6,65

Diocese: Alborg

YEAR	CHURCH ATTENDANCE	POPULATION - CHURCH ATTENDANCE	POPULATION + CHURCH ATTENDANCE	TOTAL POPULATION	PERCENTAGE
1927	22.663,6	214.968	161.646	376.614	10,54
1931	24.881,0	280.883	105.929	386.812	8,86
1935	24.937,5	259.321	124.876	384.197	9,62
1939	23.531,9	261.731	134.380	396.111	8,99
1943	22.897,9	274.832	136.088	410.920	8,33
1947	25.035,5	311.160	122.784	433.944	8,05
1951	23.139,6	299.217	134.560	433.777	7,73
1955	22.109,2	317.975	126.914	444.889	6,95
1959	19.145,1	305.909	150.799	456.708	6,52
1963	18.910,7	316.016	149.810	465.826	5,98
1967	17.540,4	366.424	113.884	480.308	4,79

Diocese: Arhus

YEAR	CHURCH ATTENDANCE	POPULATION - CHURCH ATTENDANCE	POPULATION + CHURCH ATTENDANCE	TOTAL POPULATION	PERCENTAGE
1927	21.735,0	214.520	225.553	440.073	10,13
1931	21.963,6	264.110	191.655	455.765	8.32
1935	22.356,2	289.627	172.815	462.442	7,72
1939	20,252,6	290.105	183.306	473.411	6,98
1943	18.917,6	308.601	176.436	485.037	6,13
1947	21.849,4	347.615	171.626	519.241	6,29
1951	19.334,4	325.837	197.934	523.771	5,93
1955	17.408,3	321.405	223.155	544.560	5,42
1959	14.867,2	315.629	245.052	560.681	4,71
1963	15.020,7	336.592	239.013	575.605	4,46
1967	15.758,1	383.944	220.066	604.010	4,10

YEAR	CHURCH ATTENDANCE	POPULATION - CHURCH ATTENDANCE	POPULATION + CHURCH ATTENDANCE	TOTAL POPULATION	PERCENTAGE
Diocese: Lolland-Falsters					
1927	4.804,3	71.055	58.331	129.386	6,75
1931	5.307,7	91,193	44.596	135.789	5,82
1935	5.199,5	90.797	44.897	135.694	5,73
1939	5.593,2	119.210	13.953	133.163	4,69
1943	4.769,2	107.471	26.518	133.989	4,44
1947	5.249,7	129.126	7.154	136.281	4,07
1951	4.796,1	126.592	9.733	136.325	3,79
1955	4.949,6	134.555	2.443	134.998	3,60
1959	4.398,6	128.847	6.206	135.053	3,41
1963	4.336,3	128.175	4.443	132.618	3,38
1967	3.698,2	107.723	22.582	130.305	3,43
Diocese: Ribe					
1927	20.238,8	172.125	95.187	267.312	11,76
1931	19.570,3	203.638	72.269	275.907	9,61
1935	20.489,0	216.589	59.828	276.417	9,46
1939	17.903,5	204.504	78.148	282.652	8,76
1943	17.998,2	225.988	64.795	290.783	7,96
1947	18.116,2	233.254	76.801	310.055	7,77
1951	17.639,2	253.220	57.901	311.121	6,97
1955	16.370,0	241.734	80.187	321.921	6,77
1959	16.526,6	257.908	75.173	333.081	6,41
1963	14.428,3	236.972	99.539	336.511	6,09
1967	14.791,2	252.702	97.347	350.049	5,85
Diocese: Roskilde					
1927	20.900,0	260.610	142.445	403.055	8,02
1931	22.093,9	314.044	95.450	409.494	7,04
1935	19.611,3	299.824	120.182	411.006	6,74
1939	17.216,2	291.836	120.027	411.863	5,90
1943	17.002,5	314.972	106.111	421.083	5,40
1947	18.191,9	337.854	89.348	427.202	5,38
1951	17.352,5	358.634	69.680	428.314	4,84
1955	16.235,1	357.209	86.052	443.261	4,54
1959	15.074,6	352.000	99.042	451.042	4.28
1963	14.326,4	352.121	112.439	464.560	4.07
1967	13.907,4	368.342	124.880	493.222	3,78

C. MEMBERSHIP STATISTICS IN SCANDINAVIA

DENMARK

Baptists	Methodists	Mission Covenant
1901 - 3,812	1901 - 3,895	1952 - 1,759
1910 - 4,113	1911 - 4,284	1957 - 1,759
1915 - 4,227	1921 - 4,858	1962 - 1,957
1920 - 4,913	1952 - 3,300	1968 - 1,954
1925 - 5,700	1957 - 3,500	
1930 - 5,700	1962 - 3,500	Nazarenes
1935 - 6,209	1969 - 3,232	
1940 - 6,690		1962 - 20
1945 - 6,930	Pentecostals	1963 - 22
1950 - 7,240		1964 - 21
1955 - 7,265	1910 - 200	1965 - 31
1960 - 7,185	1957 - 4,000	1966 - 31
1965 - 7,193	1970 - 4,000	1967 - 28
1970 - 7,022		1968 - 32
		1969 - 30

FINLAND

Baptists	Methodists	Mission Covenant (Free Evangelical Church of Finland)
1900 - 2,851	1900 - 319	
1910 - 4,467	1910 - 1,910	1911 - 1,500
1920 - 5,121	1929 - 2,511	1915 - 1,700
1930 - 3,561	1950 - 2,088	1922 - 1,700
1950 - 1,845	1966 - 1,889	1928 - 3,400
1962 - 1,883	1969 - 1,886	1940 - 5,000
1966 - 1,969		1950 - 5,800
1968 - 1,949	Salvation Army	1962 - 7,800
		1968 - 8,226
	1940 - 11,906	
	1945 - 10,755	
Pentecostals	1950 - 11,659	
	1955 - 10,756	
1965 - 40,000	1960 - 10,723	
1970 - 35,000	1965 - 10,909	
	1970 - 10,589	

NORWAY

Baptists	Methodists	Mission Covenant
1950 - 8,964	1950 - 11,570	1900 - 2,000
1952 - 7,360	1968 - 11,196	1910 - 2,500
1957 - 7,400	1969 - 11,342	1930 - 3,000
1962 - 7,050		1935 - 4,000
1968 - 6,650		1940 - 6,000
		1945 - 8,000
Salvation Army	**Pentecostals**	1952 - 8,340
		1957 - 8,340
1950 - 13,739	1930 - 8,000	1968 -10,500
1955 - 13,790	1960 -40,000	
1960 - 13,658	1970 -40,000	
1965 - 13,326		
1970 - 12,688		

SWEDEN

Baptists	Methodists	Mission Covenant
1900 - 40,759	1900 - 17,390	1930 - 113,000
1909 - 49,798	1905 - 17,067	1937 - 111,000
1919 - 59,515	1910 - 17,536	1957 - 99,844
1929 - 63,310	1915 - 16,384	1962 - 99,626
1939 - 49,090	1920 - 17,244	1969 - 88,000
1949 - 38,430	1925 - 16,798	
1959 - 33,077	1930 - 15,813	
1969 - 26,717	1935 - 14,618	**Salvation Army**
	1940 - 13,386	
Nazarenes	1945 - 12,341	1954 - 41,000
	1950 - 11,371	1959 - 42,000
1967 - 7	1955 - 11,643	1963 - 40,400
1968 - 8	1960 - 11,060	1964 - 41,000
1969 - 6	1965 - 8,917	1969 - 36,721
	1969 - 7,640	

Pentecostals

Evangelical Mission Foundation

Pentecostals	Evangelical Mission Foundation
1925 - 25,000	1954 - 60,000
1930 - 50,000	1959 - 50,000
1957 - 92,000	1963 - 45,000
1969 - 90,000	1964 - 40,000
	1969 - 28,586

D. ANNUAL RELIGIOUS CHANGE IN SCANDINAVIA

DENMARK 1967

AFFILIATION	ADHERENTS	(0,7%) NATURAL INCREASE	CONVERSION INCREASE	TOTAL
STATE CHURCH:				
Ev.Lutheran	4,517,000	31,619	-33,292	-1,673
FREE CHURCHES:				
Baptists	7,193	28	-42	-14
Methodists	3,536	14	-21	-7
Mission Cov.	1,954	8	-47	-39
Pentecostals	4,000	16	-32	-16*
Salvation Army	2,809	11	-30	-19*
German Ref.	70	0	0	0
Moravians	276	1	-2	-1
Adventists	4,030	16	-32	-16
Quakers	53	0	-1	-1
Nazarenes	31	0	-1	-1
OTHERS	237,955	1,595	(29,900)	(31,495)
TOTAL	4,755,698	33,292	0	33,292

*Estimates

NORWAY 1960

AFFILIATION	ADHERENTS	(0,7%) NATURAL INCREASE	CONVERSION INCREASE	TOTAL
STATE CHURCH:				
Ev.Lutheran	3,155,323	18,931	-28,108	-9,177
FREE CHURCHES:				
Baptists	9,315	56	-91	-35
Methodists	11,196	67	-104	-37
Mission Covenant	10,500	74	254	180
Pentecostals	40,000	280	-560*	-280
Salvation Army	13,658	82	-109	-27
Ev.Luth.Free Ch.	16,773	101	-120*	-19
Adventists	5,272	32	-49	-17
Quakers	208	1	-14	-13
Anglicans	494	2	-25	-23
CATHOLICS	7,875	47	359	312
ORTHODOX	610	3	-28	-25
OTHERS	352,682	2,469	(9,531)	(12,145)
TOTAL	3,707,967	22,145	0	22,145

*Estimates

FINLAND 1966

AFFILIATION	ADHERENTS	(0,6%) NATURAL INCREASE	CONVERSION INCREASE	TOTAL
STATE CHURCHES:				
Ev.Lutheran	4,362,921	26,174	-47,848	-21,674
Orthodox	68,669	415	-2,237	-1,822
FREE CHURCHES:				
Baptists	1,949	12	-42	-30
Methodists	1,886	12	-41	-29
Mission Cov.=				
(Free Evang.Ch.)	8,226	49	160	207
Pentecostals	35,000	210	-1,210	-1,000
Salvation Army	10,700	64	-164	-100
Free Lutheran	1,135	7	-32	-25
Swedish Lutheran	2,360	14	-38	-24
Anglicans	200	1	-21	-20
Adventists	4,632	28	-305	-277
CATHOLICS:				
Roman Catholics	2,689	16	35	57
Greec Catholics	1,464	9	-71	-62
Free Catholics	155	0	-7	-7
OTHERS	264,675	1,387	(1,670)	(3,057)
TOTAL	4,600,000	28,387	0	28,387

AFFILIATION	ADHERENTS	(0,4%) NATURAL INCREASE	CONVERSION INCREASE	TOTAL
STATE CHURCH:				
Ev.Lutheran	7,505,559	30,020	-40,020*	-10,000*
FREE CHURCHES:				
Baptists	26,717	108	-1,141	-1,033
Methodists	7,640	36	-1 122	-1,086
Swedish Miss.Cov.	88,000	352	-4,227	-3,875
Pentecostals	90,000	3,640	-4,640	-1,000
Salvation Army	36,721	152	-1,007	-855
Orebro Mission	19,292	76	-1,218	-1,142
Alliance Mission	13,811	56	-114	-58
Nat.Ev.Foundation	28,586	116	-1,116	-1,000
Free Baptists	1,300	4	-33	-29
Holiness Association	4,330	16	-150	-134
CATHOLICS	50,000*	2,000	6,000	8,000*
OTHERS	45,000	300	(8,204)*	(7,904)*
TOTAL	7,904,000	31,616	0	31,616

*Estimates

145

APPENDIX II

THEOLOGICAL EDUCATION: A New Plan

Due to the existence of the State Church, the ecclesiastical situation in Finland is very different from that in the United States. Theological education, as a consequence, is likewise very different. One must be well acquainted with a state-church situation before he can adequately understand the special problems involved in the education of the ministry in Finland.

In brief, the situation is as follows. Because of the existence of the State Church, accredited theological education is limited to the requirements and needs of that Church. Instead of separate seminaries for ministerial training, all theological education is under state supervision and available in only one of the state universities. The theological faculty are appointed by the president of the country, and are thus required to be members of the State Church, which is Lutheran. The number of professors and lecture rooms are limited. Therefore, the number of students necessarily remains small. Even so, not all the graduates of the state-run program can find ecclesiastical jobs upon graduation since there is already a sufficient number of professional ministers for the State Church.

On the other hand, the Free Churches of Finland lack a training leadership. They need theological educators of their own to train ministers for the various Free Churches. Such educators, by definition not functioning under the State Church and thus in the State University, could not be appointed by the government. Would the people of Finland, accustomed as they are to government-appointed teachers, accept as professionally qualified theological aducators who are not so assigned? Would Free Church ministers trained by such teachers be considered inferior? Would they find so much condescension on the part of the State Church ministers that it would be difficult for them to function as spiritual and professional leaders of their flocks? Would it be possible to build a new system of theological education that would also bear a certain prestige so necessary for the morale of the Free Church minority?

As a member of the Church of the Nazarene in Finland, I have become very interested in these questions. Part of my research this year has included the relationship of the State Church of Finland to the Church of the Nazarene, of which I am a member, and to the other Free Churches of Scandinavia. As a result of my study, I have felt compelled to offer an alternative to the system of ministerial training presently carried on by my Church and to calculate as realistically as possible how the new system could be implemented.

The Nazarene Bible College of Europe

The Nazarene Bible College was founded in 1965 in an isolated village of nine hundred German-speaking people in northern Switzerland. It is international in character, the students coming from nine European countries and speaking in a variety of languages. Its stated purpose is to train European nationals for Christian work---either the pastorate or the mission field. Its administrative and teaching staff are primarily American, with a few exceptions. The academic curriculum is by design as close as possible to that of the typical liberal arts Christian college of the United States. All teaching is done in the English language, even though it is a second language for each student and often must be learned after his entrance in the college. Cultural etiquette stressed---such as table manners and behavior in church---is American in nature, so that the students learn American culture very well.

Although originally founded in order to provide a truly international education, the college has faced much criticism from its students. The stress on English they have felt to be unnecessary in an area completely outside the English-speaking world. This is especially true when they realize that the English learned is amateurish at best. There are no classmates who are native speakers of English so that assimilation might be both natural and rapid. Furthermore, students with a more advanced knowledge of English are placed in the same classes with the newly arrived students who know no English at all. Consequently, the American professors use a very simplified English to teach their classes. Thus to say that the language learning experience is of great value is to beg the question, even when granting, as some insist, that it aids the student in communicating with the American missionaries on the field. Many people in this day would feel that the missionaries ought rather to learn the language of the people than vice versa.

The students speak many different languages. Although the school is located in a German-speaking area, only five per cent of the student body speak German. This produces a "ghetto" type of situation which is unhealthy both for the students and for the school. The community around about might well feel that the school wishes to remain isolated and uncontaminated from contact with it. Also, because of the language barrier, few students participate in local evangelism, which would enable them to put into practice what they have learned in the classroom.

Coupled with the criticism of the emphasis on the English language is the stress on the adaptation to American culture. Students feel that American cultural ideals are often equated by the American missionaries with Gospel truth, and while they inwardly rebel at being coerced with theological reasons to an American cultural pattern, they feel they must adapt outwardly or risk censure or lack of recommendation for a pastoral position upon graduation.

An equally serious complaint is related to the curriculum itself. There are many excellent schools in Europe where world history and literature may be studied. The students at the Bible College have chosen to study there precisely because they want training in the Bible and because they do not want to study the Bible under government-appointed State-Church theologians in the state university. Consequently, they are very frustrated when they are required to spend valuable time in the study of secular subjects with a professor perhaps better qualified to teach them the Bible courses they so desire. The administration, on the other hand, fears that if only Bible courses are taught academic standards will fall, and the prestige of the school will suffer.

But the problems do not end with the years of residence at college. After graduation the students are sent to their own countries to be pastors. Many of them have not yet learned to preach in their native languages. They have memorized all theological terms in English and have difficulty in translating these into their native tongues. Because they have been four years in a "little America" in Switzerland, even the strongest personalities show distinct signs of Americanization and are no longer able to think creatively in presenting the Gospel to their own people. All too often they have become dependent upon the missionary's culture, his theological reasoning, and his methods of communicating the Gospel, whether these are the wisest and best for their native cultural situation or not. Even more damaging is the fact that since the students must depend upon the school for job references to their future district superintendents, they have little choice other than to follow the missionary teachers exactly, adapting themselves to their American culture and in some cases even obeying them in opposition to their own consciences.

Aside from student criticisms there are other and more weighty problems resulting from the traditional approach to theological education. The traditional system followed at present is not training enough leaders for the Church of the Nazarene in Europe. Because of the high cost per student it is unlikely that this situation will improve unless drastic changes are made. Yet, as the Church grows, the need for trained leadership grows. Should the funds from the United States fail, for some reason, to come in, the school would have to close.

Even more serious might be the charge that the people most desirable as leaders are not the ones who become students in the college. Why? It is often the more mature men, already married and with families, who are most capable of being the spiritual leaders of a congregation. They know the problems of the people, having experienced them themselves. Yet their gifts of leadership may appear too late for them to enroll in the Bible College as it now operates. But aside from the problems of training the more mature to become pastors, there are special problems connected with training only youths. They may marry unwisely, and have to drop out of the ministry as a consequence. Or they may fail ever to develop the spiritual gifts of humility and patience and wisdom so necessary for a pastor and yet revealed only in more mature people. Also, after being withdrawn from their local communities for three years, they no longer feel at home there, even though they know these people better than anyone else and even though they are desperately needed there. The local churches throughout Europe are keenly aware that when their young men graduate from the Bible college they no longer care to minister in rural parishes but choose to wait for nonexistent openings in urban pulpits. Thus there is a surplus of pastors for city churches and the rural congregations, which are more numerous, are no better off than before they sent youths to the college.

This is not meant to be critical of the College nor of the individuals. Rather it is intended to show the limitations of a system which even under the best possible circumstances necessarily extracts the student from the culture to which he is later to minister, and puts him into a situation that is essentially artificial. If he must be in a situation foreign to him, he would be better off in a student body where the majority of the students spoke their own native tongue and in a school that belonged culturally to the surrounding environment. But even that would not assure the rural congregations of an educated leadership.

Thus it is that we must look for other solutions. One that is working well in Latin America and is now being tried for the first time in Asia and in Africa is what has come to be called "theological education by extension." Under this system the mature, proven leaders of a congregation may enroll in Biblical studies identical in content and difficulty to those taught in the Bible College. They don't need to leave their homes, jobs, nor the oversight and discipline of the local congregations. They study at home in their native tongues, using special texts prepared for self-instruction. Once a week they meet with a teacher and other students in nearby villages or cities. Because the student continues working part-time---or full time, as the need may be---he doesn't require a subsidy, but rather pays a minimal fee for his studies and his books. Grants of money from the States to the Bible College or seminary are then used for the preparation of these self-instructional texts---in a number of different languages in Europe---for lessons on cassettes, and for other special materials. Small libraries must be purchased for the centers to which the students go weekly. The travel costs of the Bible College teachers to these various centers of instruction can also be paid out of these funds.

In Latin America the weekly meetings are further strengthened by a monthly visit by each student to the campus proper of the seminary or Bible school. Here the students have access to a larger library and take courses not easily taught by extension, such as English, music, etc. They are able to exchange insights and inspiration with other students and the entire faculty while here. In Europe one such central campus may have to be located in each country, or at least in each basic language area. Then once a year the entire student body---no doubt many times greater than it now is---would gather at the existing property in Switzerland for conferences, graduation, or even for special two to six-week courses. Switzerland is a popular place, and the buildings which now exist there could be in use constantly if managed wisely. It should also be the center for the production of the special self-instructional texts, for certain types of financial management, etc.

The experience in Latin America has shown that the extension system develops study habits and discipline which the traditional student often misses. The extension student is better prepared to continue his study as a pastor because he is not conditioned to a time schedule dictated by outside forces. He has a small library of his textbooks at his hand. In his weekly center meeting he has access to a library of fifty to a hundred other books, mainly of a reference nature. Special research must also draw upon the facilities of the central base---in this case the national centers---or even upon the library of the Bible College in Switzerland which he visits periodically.

Another interesting facet of the extension system which has proven valuable is the possibility of different academic levels of instruction. In Guatemala the Presbyterian Extension Seminary operates on four different academic levels—post sixth grade which grants a diploma on completing the seminary course of study, post tenth grade which grants a bachelor's degree—equivalent to a high school diploma plus two years of college—and post two or more years of university, granting a licenciatura degree which is equivalent to a doctor's degree in the United States. Each level of seminary studies requires the same number and basic content of course material. However, the more advanced the pre-seminary education has been, the more difficult the seminary course of study. Thus the course in church history for the post sixth-grade student student uses a simpler text than is used for the post-university student, yet they both study the same basic material.

In summarizing why I feel the extension system has much to offer the Church of the Nazarene in Europe I would like to list briefly its chief attributes:

1. The selection of students is on the basis of proven call rather than an assumed call. This is made more obvious through the possibilities for study granted to more mature men and women, already leaders in the local congregation.

2. The financing of the program makes it possible to train more students than is now possible.

3. The students are trained in their own languages and within their own cultural situations; their studies are therefore relevant to the local situation and they are thus prepared for rural or city pastorates, depending upon their experience. This does not imply that a rural man can never successfully fill a city pulpit, but he is taught how to minister in a rural situation. He may need additional educational experience in a city before taking a city pastorate.

4. Each student studies at his own speed and at his own academic level. Each is ordainable within his own cultural situation upon graduation.

5. The extension student develops habits of discipline

that are essential for a successful ministry.

In starting a new system, it is essential to see that prestige accrues to it so that it may be successful in what it purports to do. In certain European situations the connection with the Swiss Bible College may be sufficient. But where this is not true, it might be possible for the entire program to be related to one of the Nazarene Colleges in America. The degrees granted would be American, but the studies would be by extension in Europe, supervised by the Bible College in Switzerland, as well as by national and regional centers of instruction. Although only one or two percent of the European students are able to come to America to study, many more desire to come. The extension system would enable these students to secure quality education with even perhaps, a U. S. diploma without the expense of studying abroad and the problem of cultural displacement which it inevitably causes.

There are various technical aspects to planning an extension seminary course. These include the costs of extension versus the traditional Bible College, the location of centers of various levels, and an analysis of the need for centers country by country. Such factors are best depicted in chart or outline form. Although I do not know the exact costs of ministerial training in the Nazarene Bible College in Switzerland, I have estimated them to be somewhat as follows in Figure A. The estimated costs of an extension program may be found in Figure B. Figure C depicts the various possible sites for weekly, monthly, or annual meetings of an extension system in Europe.

Finally I am including a brief sketch of the ministry in Scandinavia. The facts of the overall situation sometimes make strategic planning more effective. They serve as guideposts as we rethink and redesign ministerial training to fit the cultural context so that more men may be led to Christ.

Figure A

Counting the Cost: European Nazarene Bible College (accurate figures have not been available, however, the figures presented are thought to be realistic.)

1. Gross Annual Cost of Institution: $67,470

2. Gross Annual Administrative and Instructional Cost:
   a) $50,000 Aid from Kansas City
      6,000 Missionary salaries
      2,500 Aid from European churches
      8,960 Tuition (35 students; $8.00 per unit; 1120 units per year)
      (8,750) Room and Board per year; 35 students
   $76,470

3. Gross Annual Administrative and Instructional Cost per student: $1,920

4. Cost per units taken: $60.24

5. Cost per Student Study Hour: $30.10

6. Student Study hours per Staff-Teacher Hours: (2.8) 3 hrs

7. Cost per Graduate (Average of 5 graduates per year): $13,494

8. Cost per Ordained Minister. (Average of 3 graduates per year likely to take pastorate) $22,490

9. Foreign Subsidy Cost: 7.5%

(Note: these nine categories are explained in detail in
THEOLOGICAL EDUCATION BY EXTENSION,
by Ralph D. Winter, 1969: 439-441.)

Figure B

Counting the Cost---Extension

This has been calculated with the country of Finland in mind. Since the State theological schools are overcrowded and many are turned away, I assume that the Nazarenes would find it successful to operate Theological Education by Extension. Especially it would add prestige, if an existing Nazarene College here would grant degrees (Th.B.) Natutally this will not compare with the University in Helsinki, but it will be better than nothing and far better than all the other institutions outside the University, which do not grant degrees.

1 & 2   Gross Annual Administrative and Instructional Cost: $2,940.00

3   Gross Annual Administrative and Instructional Cost per Student: $16.80

4   Cost per Unit Taken: $1.68

5   Cost per Student Study Hour: $0.84

6   Student Study Hours per Staff-Teacher Hours: 0.28

7   Cost per Graduate: (Average 44 per year; 25%;) $66.80

8   Cost per Ordained Minister. (Average 22 graduates per year) $133.60

9   Foreign Subsidy Cost: 3.1%

Figure C

A Tentative Plan for an Indigenous
Nazarene Theological Education Project in Europe

Home (Daily)
w Extension Center (Weekly)
(M) Regional Center (Monthly)
■ Headquarters (Annual) Switzerland

A Brief Sketch of the Ministry in Scandinavia

SWEDEN:

1. The total number of Priests in the State Church (Lutheran) in 1963 was 2,700; that is, one to every 2,740 inhabitants.
2. In 1980 half of the priests will be retired. Today, 400 new priests are needed yearly.
3. Recruitment: a) The State Church now ordains ex-Salvation Army officers, ex-missionaries, ex-free church pastors, social workers, etc., after a brief theological orientation. They will be full-time workers having the same privileges as those graduating from the universities.

   b) Plans are that, in the near future, the Church will ordain part-time priests. They will first receive a basic theological orientation. The idea is that they will have their secular occupations and serve the Church in their free time, administering sacraments, preaching, and doing other parish work. They will be paid by the Church.

   c) Women priests. On April 10, 1960, the first three women took Holy Orders in the State Church. The decision to admit women to Holy Orders has caused the fiercest debate ever witnessed in Swedish church history. About one third of the priests are against this. The majority of the priests and the public favor women priests. Women priests enjoy the overwhelming favor of their churches. Church attendance has proved to be much higher when a women preaches. Today Sweden has forty women priests. The majority of them have an education far beyond their male colleagues.

FINLAND:

1. The total number of priests in the State Church in 1966 was 1,784; that is one to every 2,700 inhabitants.
2. In ten years 30% of the priests will be retiring.

3. Recruitment: a) Full training entails about seven years of theological study in the university. Only about 70% of those who seek entrance to the Theological School in the University pass the entrance examinations. Despite this fact, the theological department has the largest numbers of students in the University. While students in the other departments have doubled, the theological department has doubled four times. Most of the theological students are women, thus making the proportion of women theologs to the population the greatest in the world.

b) Between 1920 and 1966, thirty six men received special permission to be ordained, ex-Methodist pastors and experienced missionaries.

c) Women. Today, in 1970, there are about 700 women with theological training in the State Church; most of them are in parish work.

In Finland we are now experiencing greater interest in the ministry than ever before in the history of the country. All theological institutions, whether for training deaconesses, youth leaders, organists or whatever, are overcrowded. In the near future the existing structure of the State Church will not have places for all of the graduates.

DENMARK:

1. The total number of priests in the State Church in 1967 was 1,900; that is, one to every 2,531 inhabitants.
2. Recruitment:

   a) The priesthood is open to persons who have graduated with a degree in theology from one of the Danish universities.

   b) The priesthood is open to missionaries of foreign missions who, after having passed a special university examination, have seen at least seven years' service.

   c) The priesthood is open for priests who have, for at least seven years, served Danish Evangelical-Lutheran churches outside the Kingdom.

   d) In special cases, the priesthood can be made accessible by Royal Decree to others, e.g. to persons who have a university degree other than that in divinity.

e) A Parochial Church Council can obtain permission to have appointed as priest a person who, without having been trained in any of the ways specified above, through his work for the Church and the congregation has been found qualified for the priesthood.

All need a university course of six months in pastoral theology. Before ordination by the bishop of the diocese, the candidates for the priesthood undergo a "bishop's examination," which is less a test of their knowledge than an informative interview about the problems of the priesthood. The King appoints all permanent priests, on nomination by the Church Ministry.

f) The first ordination of women took place in 1947. To-day there are thirty women priests in Denmark.

Bibliography

AARFLOT, Andreas
1967　　NORSK KIRKEHISTORIE. Oslo, Lutherstiftelsen

AITTALA, Wiljam
1970　　Letter to the author, March 12.

ALLEN, Harold
1969　　Letter to the author, November 14.

ALLEN, Roland
1962　　MISSIONARY METHODS: ST PAUL'S OR OURS?
　　　　Grand Rapids, Michigan, William B. Eerdmans
　　　　Publishing Company.

1965a　THE MINISTRY OF THE SPIRIT. Grand Rapids,
　　　　Michigan, William B. Eerdmans Publishing
　　　　Company.

ANDERSEN, Nils Knud and LINDHAROT, P. G.
1966　　DEN DANSKE KIRKENS HISTORIE. Vol. VIII.
　　　　Copenhagen, Nordisk Forlag.

ANDERSEN, Nils Knud and BANNING, Knud (Editors)
1969　　KIRKE HISTORISKE SAMLINGER 1969.
　　　　Copenhagen, Gec Cads Forlag.

ANDERSON, Gerald H. (Editor)
1965　　THE THEOLOGY OF THE CHRISTIAN MISSION.
　　　　New York, McGraw-Hill Company.

ANTTURI, Kai
1970　　Letter to the author, February 19.

ARDEN, Everett G.
1964　　FOUR NORTHERN LIGHTS. Men Who Shaped
　　　　Scandinavian Churches. Minneapolis, Minnesota,
　　　　Augsburg Publishing House.

ASP, Erkki
  1965   LAPPALAISET JA LAPPALAISUUS.   Turku,
          Turun Yliopiston julkaisuja, Sarja C, osa 2.

BAVINCK, J. H.
  1960   AN INTRODUCTION TO THE SCIENCE OF
          MISSIONS.   Philadelphia, Pennsylvania, The
          Presbyterian and Reformed Publishing Company.

BEAVER, R. Pierce
  1967   TO ADVANCE THE GOSPEL.   Grand Rapids,
          Michigan,   William B. Eerdmans Publishing
          Company.

BENGTSON, Bo and CEDERGREN, Hugo
  1953   PRINS OSCAR BERNADOTTE.   Uppsala, J.A.
          Lindblads Forlag.

BENNETT, John Coleman
  1958   CHRISTIANS AND THE STATE.
          New York, Scribner.

BERGROTH, Elis
  1902   SUOMEN KIRKKO.   Sen Kehitys, sen vaikutus
          kansaan ja sen suhde valtioon.   Porvoo, WSOY.

BLOCH-HOELL, Nils
  1964   THE PENTECOSTAL MOVEMENT
          Oslo, Universitetforlaget.
          (Norwegian Edition 1956)

BOER, Harry
  1964   PENTECOST AND MISSIONS.   Grand Rapids,
          Michigan,   William B. Eerdmans Publishing
          Company.

BRADSHAW, Malcolm R.
  1969   CHURCH GROWTH THROUGH EVANGELISM-
          IN - DEPTH.   South Pasadena, California,
          William Carey Library.

BUTTERFIELD, Herbert
   1951   CHRISTIANITY IN EUROPEAN HISTORY.
            London, William Collins Sons Company.

BIBLE CLUB MOVEMENT, Inc.
   1969   Pamphlets.

BIBLE CHRISTIAN UNION
   1969   Pamphlets.

BRUCKS, George A.
   1970   Letter to the author, March 6.

CAMPUS CRUSADE FOR CHRIST, INTERNATIONAL
   1969   Reports and Pamphlets.

CARLSSON, Sten and ROSEN, Jecker
   1961   SVENSK HISTORIA II.
            Stockholm, Svenska Bokforlaget

CHILD EVANGELISM FELLOWSHIP
   1969   Pamphlets

CHRISTIE, H. C.
   1945   DEN NORSKE KIRKE I KAMP.
            Oslo, Land og Kirke.

CONRAD, W. Howard
   1967   "A Report to the Department of World Mission
            of the Church of the Church of the Nazarene concerning Growth
            on its Mission Fields." An unpublished M.A.
            Thesis, Fuller Theological Seminary.

COOPER, Clay
   1965   NOTHING TO WIN BUT THE WORLD.
            Grand Rapids, Michigan, Zondervan.

COXHILL, H. Wakelin and GRUBB, Kenneth (Editors)
   1957   WORLD CHRISTIAN HANDBOOK.   London,
   1967   Lutterworth Press.

DAWSON, Christopher
1968   THE MAKING OF EUROPE.
        New York, World Publishing Company.

DET NORSKE BAPTISTSAMFUNN
1969   Oslo, Arbok 1969.

DURNBAUGH, Donald F.
1969   GUDSFOLK OCH FOLKKYRKA.
        Lund, Gleerups Forlag.

ERIKSON, J. M.
1895   METODISMEN I SVERIGE.
        Stockholm, K. J. Bohlins Forlag.

EVANKELISLUTERILAISEN SISÄLÄHETYSSÄÄTIÖN
1968   TOIMINTAKERTOMUS

EVANS, Robert P.
1963   LET EUROPE HEAR.   Chicago, Moody Press.

FILADELFIAFORSAMLINGEN I STOCKHOLM
1970   Letter to the author, February 18.

GJERSET, Knud
1915   HISTORY OF THE NORWEGIAN PEOPLE.
        New York, The Macmillan Company.

GODDARD, Burton L.
1967   THE ENCYCLOPEDIA OF MODERN CHRISTIAN
        MISSIONS, New Jersey, Thomas Nelson & Sons.

GREENWAY, Roger S.
1970   'Training Urban Church Planters in Latin
        America.'   CHURCH GROWTH BULLETIN.
        VI : 3: 38-43.

GUSTAFSSON, Berndt.
1965   "Church and People" in SVENSKA INSTITUT,
        October, 1965.

Bibliography

GUSTAFSSON, Berndt
  1963   "The Christian Faith in Sweden,"
          October, 1963, SVENSKA INSTITUT.

HAAVIO, Ari
  1965   SUOMEN USKONNOLLISET LIIKKEET. Porvoo,
          Werner, Soderstrom Osakeyhtio.

HÅLAND, Carl
  1963.   VAST SVENSKA KYRKA. Lund, Sleerups
          Forlag.

HALLENDORFF, Carl and SCHUCK, Adolf
  1938   HISTORY OF SWEDEN. London, Cassell and
          Company.

HÄMÄLÄINEN, Aapeli
  1970   Letter to the author, March 17.

HAMILTON, J. Taylor
  1901   A HISTORY OF THE MISSIONS OF THE
          MORAVIAN CHURCH. Bethlehem, Penna.
          Times Publishing Company.

HARR, Wilber Christian (Editor)
  n.d.   FRONTIER OF THE CHRISTIAN WORLD MIS-
          SION SINCE 1938. Chicago, Association of
          Professors of Missions.

HARTLING, Poul, (Editor)
  1964   THE DANISH CHURCH.
          Copenhagen, Det Danske Selskab.
          (Translated by Sigurd Mammen)

HARVEY, William L. and REPPIEN, Christian
  1915   DENMARK AND THE DANES.
          London, Fisher Unwin Company .

HELLSTEN, Erik G.
  1970   Letter to the author, January 16.

HENRY, Carl F. H. and MOONEYHAM, W. Stanley (Eds)
1967   ONE RACE, ONE GOSPEL, ONE TASK. Vols. I
        and II.   Minneapolis, World Wide Publications.

HENRY, A. M.
1962   A MISSION THEOLOGY. Notre Dame, Indiana.

HERMAN, Stewart Winfield
1953   REPORT FROM CHRISTIAN EUROPE,
        New York, Friendship Press.

HILLERDAL, Gunnar and PETREN, Erik
1967   EN FRIKYRKA. Uppsala, Medborgarskolan.

HILTUNEN, Paavo
1970   "Jumala ompi linnamme jäätyi Senaatintorilla"
        UUSI TIE. Tammikuu.

HODGES, Melvin L.
1970   "Surmounting Seven Obstacles to Church Growth"
        CHURCH GROWTH BULLETIN. VI: 3:43-45.

HODGES, Melvin L.
1953   THE INDIGENOUS CHURCH.
        Springfield, Gospel Publishing House.

HOFFMAN, Gerhard
1969   "Considerations on Integration of Church and
        Mission in Germany."
        INTERNATIONAL REVIEW OF MISSIONS.
        LXIII: (July) 278-291.

HOLMQUIST, Hjalmar
1938   SVENSKA KYRKANS HISTORIA. Vol. IV.
        Stockholm, Svenska Kyrkans Diakoniastyrelses
        Bokforlag.

HONKANEN, Eino (and others)
1967   TOTTELIN TAIVAALLISTA NÄKYÄ. Urho
        Muroman Muistokirja. Porvoo, WSOY.

HUNTER, Leslie Stannard (Editor)
1965   SCANDINAVIAN CHURCHES. Minneapolis,
        Minnesota, Augsburg Publishing House.

JENSEN, Arne
1961   BAPTISTERNAS HISTORIE I DANMARK INDTIL
        1864. Copenhagen,
        Baptisternas Forlag.

JOHNSON, Jerry
1962   EXPLORATION-DENMARK. Kansas City,
        Missouri, Nazarene Publishing House.

JUTIKKA, Eino and PIRINEN, Kauko
1962.   HISTORY OF FINLAND.
        London, Thames and Hudson.
        (Translated by Paul Sjöblom.)

JUVA, Einar Wilhelm
1964-67   SUOMEN KANSAN HISTORIA. Helsinki, Otava

KANKAINEN, Kosti
1967   "Taistelu Jumalan vihreista niityista" in Eino
        Honkanen (and others) TOTTELIN TAIVAAL-
        LISTA NAKYA, Porvoo, WSOY

KANSAN RAAMATTUSEURAN SÄÄTIÖ
1969   Pamphlets.

KARES, Olavi
1941-47   HERÄNNEEN KANSAN VAELLUS. Vol. I-IV.
           Helsinki.
1963   KIRKKOLAIVAN KÖLIVESILLA. Porvoo, WSOY

KARHU, Sinikka
1970   Letter to the author, February 17.

KELLER, Adolph
1942   CHRISTIAN EUROPE TODAY.
        New York, Harper & Brothers

KIK, Jacob Marcellus
1958   ECUMENISM AND THE EVANGELICAL. Phila-
         delphia, Presbyterian & Reformed Publishing
         Company.

KIRKON KALENTERI
1969   Helsinki, Suomen kirkon Sisalahetysseura.

KOCH, Hal
1949   DANMARKS KIRKE GENNEM TIDERNE.
         Copenhagen, Gyldendal Forlag.

KOCH, Hal and KORNERUP, Bjorn
1950-66 DEN DANSKE KIRKENS HISTORIE. Vols. I-
         VIII. Copenhagen, Nordisk Forlag.

KONONEN, Elsa
1964   HENGEN MIEKKA, AUTTAVA KASI.
         Porvoo, WSOY.

KOIRANEN, Vilho A.
1966   SUOMALAISTEN SIIRTOLAISTEN SULAUTU-
         MINEN RUOTSISSA. Porvoo, WSOY.

KOSKELAINEN, Osmo
1968   MAALLISTUVA SUOMALAINEN SUURKAU-
         PUNKI. Porvoo, WSOY.

KUOPPALA, Jussi
1970   Letter to the author, March 24.

LANG, Bernt. C. (Editor.)
1966   NORSK KIRKEHISTORIE. Lutherstiftelsen.

KAUVENG, Kare
1970   Letter to the author, February 18.

LATOURETTE, Kenneth Scott
1959   THE NINETEENTH CENTURY IN EUROPE.
         Vol. II. Grand Rapids, Michigan, Zondervan

1961   THE TWENTIETH CENTURY IN EUROPE.
        Grand Rapids, Michigan, Zondervan.

LAVIK, Johannes
1949   SPENNINGEN I NORSK KIRKELIV.
        Oslo, Gyldendal Norsk Forlag.

LEWIS, Arthur James
1962   ZINZENDORF, THE ECUMENICAL PIONEER.
        Philadelphia, Westminster Press.

LINDSELL, Harold
1949   A CHRISTIAN PHILOSOPHY OF MISSIONS.
        Wheaton, Illinois, Van Kampen Press.
1962   "Faith Missions Since 1938," in Wilbur C. Harr
        (Ed) FRONTIER OF THE CHRISTIAN WORLD
        MISSION SINCE 1938, pp. 189-230.

LINDESTAD, Anna-Stina
1970   Letter to the author, March 17.

LUNDMARK, Gust.
1970   Letter to the author, January 23.

METODISTIKIRON SUOMEN VUOSIKONFERENSSIN
1969.   VUOSIKIRJA.

METODISTKIRKENS ÅRSKONFERANCE I NORGE,
1969   Oslo.

METODISTKYRKANS IN FINLAND SVENSKA ÅRSBOK,
1969   Helsinki.

METODISTKYRKANS I SVERIGE ÅRSBOK.
1969   Stockholm.

MOLLAND, Einar
1957   CHURCH LIFE IN NORWAY. Minneapolis,
        Augsburg Publishing House. (Translated by
        Harris Kaasa).

1968   FRA HANS NIELSEN HAUGE TIL EIVIND
         BERGGRAV. Oslo, Gyldendal Norsk Forlag.

MORLEY, Frank W.
1970.   Letter to the author, January 20.

MURRAY, Robert
1961   A BRIEF HISTORY OF THE CHURCH OF
         SWEDEN, Stockholm, Diakoniastyrelsens BF.

MURRAY, Albert Victor
1958   THE STATE AND THE CHURCH IN A FREE
         SOCIETY. Cambridge, University Press.

MURTORINNE, Eino
1967   TAISTELU UNSKONNONVAPAUDESTA.
         Porvoo, WSOY.

MC GAVRAN, Donald A.
1957   THE BRIDGES OF GOD.
         New York, Friendship Press.

1959a   HOW CHURCHES GROW.
         New York, Friendship Press.

1965b   CHURCH GROWTH AND CHRISTIAN MISSION.
         New York, Harper & Row.

1970c   UNDERSTANDING CHURCH GROWTH.
         Grand Rapids, Michigan, William B. Eerdmans
         Publishing Company.

NEILL, Stephen
1965   A HISTORY OF CHRISTIAN MISSIONS.
         Grand Rapids, Michigan
         William B. Eerdmans Publishing Company.

NEWMAN, Ernst
1932   "Hedbergianismen i Sverige." Acta Academiae
         Aboensis Humaniora. Abo Academi, VIII, 1-200

NIDA, Eugene A.
   1954   CUSTOMS AND CULTURES.
             New York, Harper & Row.

   1960   MESSAGE AND MISSION.
             New York, Harper & Row.

   1968   RELIGION ACROSS CULTURES.
             New York, Harper & Row.

NODTVEDT, Magnus
   1965   REBIRTH OF NORWAY'S PEASANTRY. Folk
             Leader Hans Nielsen Hauge.   Tacoma, Wash.
             Pacific Lutheran University Press.

THE NORWAY YEAR BOOK, 1967.
   1966   Oslo, Johan Gundt Tanun Forlag.

NORWOOD, Frederick A.
   1954   THE DEVELOPMENT OF MODERN CHRIS-
             TIANITY.   New York,   Abingdon Press.

NORTH AMERICAN PROTESTANT MINISTRIES OVERSEAS
             DIRECTORY   8TH EDITION.
   1968   Waco, Texas. Word Books.

NYHLEN, Erik
   1964   SVENSK FRIKYRKA.
             Stockholm, Bokforlaget Prisma.

OLSON, Arnold Theodore
   1964   BELIEVERS ONLY. Minneapolis, Free Church
             Publications.

ORR, J. Edwin
   1949   THE SECOND EVANGELICAL AWAKENING IN
             BRITAIN. London, Marshall, Morgan & Scott.

   1965a   THE LIGHT OF THE NATIONS. Grand Rapids,
             William B. Eerdmans Publishing Company.

1968b   THE WILLING VOICE, Mission to the Academic Community, Pasadena, California.

PETERSEN, Wilhelm
1921   THE LIGHT IN THE PRISON WINDOW. Minneapolis, Minnesota. K.C.Holter Publishing Company.

RASMUSSEN, Carl C.
1948   WHAT ABOUT SCANDINAVIA? Philadelphia, Muhlenberg Press.

READ, William R.
1965   NEW PATTERNS OF CHURCH GROWTH IN BRAZIL. Grand Rapids, Michigan, William B. Eerdmans Publishing Company.

READ, W. R., MONTERROSO, V. M., JOHNSON, H. A.,
1969   LATIN AMERICAN CHURCH GROWTH. William B. Eerdmans Publishing Company.

RICHARDSON, William J.
1966   REVOLUTION IN MISSIONARY THINKING. Maryknoll, New York, Maryknoll Publications.

RUUTH, Martti
1909   "Uskonnollinen separatismi ja uskonnonvapautta koskeva lainsäädäntö Suomessa." OMA MAA. Vol. IV. 782-792.

ROSENQIST, G. O.
1952   SUOMEN KIRKON MURROSAIKOJA. Porvoo, WSOY. (Translated by Niilo Syvanne).

ROSS, Irwin
1962   "Is Finland Playing Russian Roulette?" Reader's Digest, 1962: (December) 197-204.

SALMENSAARI, S. S.
1957   SUOMEN VAPAAKIRKKO. Tampere, Paiva.

SALOMIES, Ilmari
1964   Jumalantulet. Porvoo, WSOY.

SANDALL, Robert
1947   THE HISTORY OF THE SALVATION ARMY.
          Vols. I, III. London, Thomas Nelson and Sons,

SCHMIDT, Wolfgang
1940   FINLANDS KYRKA GENOM TIDERNA.
          Stockholm, Svenska kyrkans Diakoniastyrelsen
          Bokforlag.

SCHARPFF, Paulus
1964   HISTORY OF EVANGELISM. Grand Rapids,
          Michigan, William B. Eerdmans Publishing
          Company. (Translated by Helga Bender Henry
          from the original German.)

SCHWARZ, David
1966   SVENSKA MINORITETER.
          Stockholm, Bokforlaget Aldus Bonniers.

SCOTT, Nova M.
1970   Letter to the author, February 19.

SEAMANDS, John T.
1964   THE SUPREME TASK OF THE CHURCH.
          Grand Rapids, Michigan, William B. Eerdmans
          Publishing Company.

SENTZE, Geert
1963   FINLAND, ITS CHURCH AND ITS PEOPLE.
          Helsinki.

SHERILL, Henry Knox
1949   THE CHURCH'S MINISTRY IN OUR TIME.
          New York, Charles Scribner's Sons.

SIMOJOKI, Martti
1958   KIRKKO JA MAAILMA. Porvoo, WSOY.

1960   KIRKKO JA NYKYAIKA. Porvoo, WSOY.

SMALLEY, William A.
1958   "Cultural Implications of an Indigenous Church."
         PRACTICAL ANTHROPOLOGY. 5: 51-65

SMITH, Catherine Ruth
1970   Letter to the author, February 20.

SNYDER, Louis
1954   THE MEANING OF NATIONALISM.
         New Brunswick, Rutgers University Press.

SOMMERSETH, H.
1970   Letter to the author, February 21.

STATISTISK ÅRSBOK FOR SVERIGE, ÅRGANG 54.
1967   Stockholm, Statistiska Centralbyran, 1967.

STIANSEN, Peder
1933   HISTORY OF THE BAPTISTS IN NORWAY.
         Chicago, Blessing Press.

SUNDKLER, Bengt
1965   THE WORLD OF MISSION. London, Lutterworth.

SVANELL, Elon
1970   Letter to the author, February 18.

SVENSKA KYRKANS ÅRSBOK, 1970.
1969   Stockholm, AB Verbum-Kyrkliga Centralforlaget

SVENSKA MISSIONSFÖRBUNDET
1969   Pamphlets

SUOMEN EVANKELISLUTERILAINEN KIRKKO VUOSINA
1968   1962-1966

SALVATION ARMY YEARBOOKS, 1935-1969. London,
         Salvationist Publishing and Supplies, Ltd.

TALVITIE, Simo, (Editor)
1957   MIES JUMALAN LÄHETTÄMÄ. Ystävien kirja
        Frank Mangsista. Helsinki, Kuva ja Sana.

THOMPSON, Augustus C.
1882   MORAVIAN MISSIONS.
        New York, Charles Scribner's Sons.

THYSSEN, Anders P.
1960-67 VAEKKELSERNAS FREMBRUD I DANMARK
        I FØRSTE HALVDEL AV DET 19 ARHUND-
        REDE.
        Copenhagen, Gec Cads Forlag.

TIPPETT, A. R.
1966   "Church Growth or Else!" WORLD VISION
        MAGAZINE. (February) pp. 12, 28.
1969   VERDICT THEOLOGY IN MISSIONARY THEORY.
        Illinois, Lincoln Christian College Press.

TIILIKAINEN, Mauri
1969   Letter to the author, December 18.

TOLAMO, Marha-Terttu
1968   Interview with the author, August.
1969   Letter to the author, December 19.

UNGER, Monte C.
1970   Letter to the author, February 19.

UUSI TIE, 46: 1969; 12   Helsinki

VÄISÄNEN, Matti
1969   "Herra lähetä minut." VIE SANOMA. 1969:18-20.

VAINIKAINEN, Kerttu
1968   Interview with the author, July.

VÄLIAHO, Juha
1970   Letter to the author, February 27.

VANHA-PERTTULA, Veikko
    1949   "Urho Muromasta ja hänen evankelioimistyö-
            stään." An unpublished M.A. thesis, University
            of Helsinki.

VEHMAS, Raino
    1961   SUOMEN ROMAANIVÄESTON RYHMÄLUONNE
            JA AKKULTUROITUMINEN.   Turku, Turun
            Yliopiston julkaisuja, B: 81.

VISSER T'HOOFT, W.A.
    1963   NO OTHER NAME. London, S.C.M. Press.

WESTIN, Gunnar
    1958   THE FREE CHURCH THROUGH THE AGES.
            Nashville, Tennessee, Broadman Press.
            (Translated by Virgil A. Olson.)

WINTER, Ralph D. (Editor)
    1969   THEOLOGICAL EDUCATION BY EXTENSION.
            South Pasadena, California,   William Carey
            Library.

    1969a   "The Anatomy of the Christian Mission."
            EVANGELICAL MISSIONS QUARTERLY.
            5: 2; 74-89

WISELIUS, Ingemar
    1967   SWEDEN IN THE SIXTIES.
            Stockholm, Svenska Institut.

WUMBELMANN, Knud
    1970   Letter to the author, February 24.

Index

William Carey Library
PUBLICATIONS

Africa

PEOPLES OF SOUTHWEST ETHIOPIA, by A. R. Tippett,Ph.D.
A recent, penetrating evaluation by a professional anthropologist of the cultural complexities faced by Peace Corps workers and missionaries in a rapidly changing intersection of African states.
1970: 320 pp, $3.95. ISBN 0-87808-103-8

PROFILE FOR VICTORY: NEW PROPOSALS FOR MISSIONS IN ZAMBIA, by Max Ward Randall.
"In a remarkably objective manner the author has analyzed contemporary political, social educational and religious trends, which demand a reexamination of traditional missionary methods and the creation of daring new strategies...his conclusions constitute a challenge for the future of Christian missions, not only in Zambia, but around the world."
1970: 224 pp, Cloth, $3.95. ISBN 0-87808-403-7

THE CHURCH OF THE UNITED BRETHREN OF CHRIST IN SIERRA LEONE, by Emmett D. Cox, Executive Secretary, United Brethren in Christ Board of Missions.
A readable account of the relevant historical, demographic and anthropological data as they relate to the development of the United Brethren in Christ Church in the Mende and Creole communities. Includes a reformation of objectives.
1970: 184 pp, $2.95. ISBN 0-87808-301-4

APPROACHING THE NUER OF AFRICA THROUGH THE OLD TESTAMENT, by Ernest A. McFall.
The author examines in detail the similarities between the Nuer and the Hebrews of the Old Testament and suggests a novel Christian approach that does not make initial use of the New Testament.
1970: 104 pp, 8 1/2 x 11, $1.95.
ISBN 0-87808-310-3

Asia

TAIWAN: MAINLINE VERSUS INDEPENDENT CHURCH GROWTH,
A STUDY IN CONTRASTS, by Allen J. Swanson.
   A provocative comparison between the older,
historical Protestant churches in Taiwan and the
new indigenous Chinese churches; suggests stag-
gering implications for missions everywhere that
intend to promote the development of truly indigenous expressions of Christianity.
   1970: 216 pp, $2.95. ISBN 0-87808-404-5

NEW PATTERNS FOR DISCIPLING HINDUS: THE NEXT
STEP IN ANDHRA PRADESH, INDIA, by B.V. Subbamma.
   Proposes the development of a Christian movement that is as well adapted culturally to the
Hindu tradition as the present movement is to the
Harijan tradition. Nothing could be more crucial
for the future of 400 million Hindus in India
today.
   1970: 212 pp, $3.45. ISBN 0-87808-306-5

GOD'S MIRACLES: INDONESIAN CHURCH GROWTH, by Ebbie
C. Smith, Th.D.
   The fascinating details of the penetration of
Christianity into the Indonesian archipelago make
for intensely interesting reading, as the anthropological context and the growth of the Christian
movement are highlighted.
   1970: 224 pp, $3.45. ISBN 0-87808-302-2

NOTES ON CHRISTIAN OUTREACH IN A PHILIPPINE
COMMUNITY, by Marvin K. Mayers, Ph.D.
   The fresh observations of an anthropologist
coming from the outside provide a valuable, however
preliminary, check list of social and historical
factors in the context of missionary endeavors in a
Tagalog province.
   1970: 71 pp, 8 1/2 x 11, $1.45. ISBN 0-87808-104-6

Latin America

THE PROTESTANT MOVEMENT IN BOLIVIA, by C. Peter
Wagner.
   An excitingly-told account of the gradual
build-up and present vitality of Protestantism.
A cogent analysis of the various subcultures
and the organizations working most effectively,
including a striking evaluation of Bolivia's
momentous Evangelism-in-Depth year and the possibilities of Evangelism-in-Depth for other parts
of the world.
   1970: 264 pp, $3.95. ISBN 0-87808-402-9

LA SERPIENTE Y LA PALOMA, by Manuel Gaxiola.

The impressive success story of the Apostolic
Church of Mexico, (an indigenous denomination
that never had the help of any foreign missionary),
told by a professional scholar now the director
of research for that church. (Spanish)

1970: 200 pp, $2.95. ISBN 0-87808-802-4

THE EMERGENCE OF A MEXICAN CHURCH: THE ASSOCIATE
REFORMED PRESBYTERIAN CHURCH OF MEXICO, by James
Erskine Mitchell.

Tells the ninety-year story of the Associate
Reformed Presbyterian Mission in Mexico, the trials
and hardships as well as the bright side of the
work. Eminently practical and helpful regarding
the changing relationship of mission and church in
the next decade.

1970: 184 pp, $2.95. ISBN 0-87808-303-0

FRIENDS IN CENTRAL AMERICA, by Paul C. Enyart.

This book describes the results of faithful and
effective labors of the California Friends Yearly
Meeting, giving an analysis of the growth of one of
the most virile, national evangelical churches in
Central America, comparing its growth to other evangelical churches in Guatemala, Honduras, and El
Salvador.

1970: 224 pp, $3.45. ISBN 0-87808-405-3

Europe

THE CHALLENGE FOR EVANGELICAL MISSIONS TO EUROPE:
A SCANDINAVIAN CASE STUDY, by Hilkka Malaska.

Graphically presents the state of Christianity
in Scandinavia with an evaluation of the pros and
cons and possible contributions that existing or
additional Evangelical missions can make in Europe
today.

1970: 192 pp, $2.95. ISBN 0-87808-308-1

THE PROTESTANT MOVEMENT IN ITALY: ITS PROGRESS,
PROBLEMS, AND PROSPECTS, by Roger Hedlund.

A carefully wrought summary of preliminary
data; perceptively develops issues faced by Evangelical Protestants in all Roman Catholic areas of
Europe. Excellent graphs.

1970: 266 pp, $3.95. ISBN 0-87808-307-3

U.S.A.

THE YOUNG LIFE CAMPAIGN AND THE CHURCH, by Warren Simandle.

If 70 per cent of young people drop out of the church between the ages of 12 and 20, is there room for a nationwide Christian organization working on high school campuses? After a quarter of a century, what is the record of Young Life and how has its work with teens affected the church? *"A careful analysis based on a statistical survey; full of insight and challenging proposals for both Young Life and the church."*

1970: 216 pp, $3.45. ISBN 0-87808-304-9

THE RELIGIOUS DIMENSION IN SPANISH LOS ANGELES: A PROTESTANT CASE STUDY, by Clifton L. Holland.

A through analysis of the origin, development and present extent of this vital, often unnoticed element in Southern California.

1970: 304 pp, $3.95. ISBN 0-87808-309-X

General

THEOLOGICAL EDUCATION BY EXTENSION, edited by Ralph D. Winter, Ph.D.

A husky handbook on a new approach to the education of pastoral leadership for the church. Gives both theory and practice and the exciting historical development in Latin America of the *"Largest non-governmental voluntary educational development project in the world today."* Ted Ward, Prof. of Education, Michigan State University.

1969: 648 pp, Library Buckram $7.95, Kivar $4.95. ISBN 0-87808-101-1

THE CHURCH GROWTH BULLETIN, VOL. I-V, edited by Donald A. McGavran, Ph.D.

The first five years of issues of a now-famous bulletin which probes past foibles and present opportunities facing the 100,000 Protestant and Catholic missionaries in the world today. No periodical edited for this audience has a larger readership.

1969: 408 pp, Library Buckram $6.95, Kivar $4.45. ISBN 0-87808-701-X

CHURCH GROWTH THROUGH EVANGELISM-IN-DEPTH, by
Malcolm R. Bradshaw.
   *"Examines the history of Evangelism-in-Depth
and other total mobilization approaches to evangelism. Also presents concisely the 'Church
Growth' approach to mission and proposes a
wedding between the two...a great blessing to the
church at work in the world." WORLD VISION
MAGAZINE.*
   1969: 152 pp, $2.45. ISBN 0-87808-401-0

THE TWENTY FIVE UNBELIEVABLE YEARS, 1945-1969, by
Ralph D. Winter, Ph.D.
   A terse, exciting analysis of the most significant transition in human history in this millenium
and its impact upon the Christian movement. *"Packed
with insight and otherwise unobtainable statistical
data...a brilliant piece of work."* C. Peter Wagner.
   1970: 120 pp, $1.95. ISBN 0-87808-102-X

EL SEMINARIO DE EXTENSION: UN MANUAL, by James H.
Emery, F. Ross Kinsler, Louise J. Walker, Ralph D.
Winter.
   Gives the reasons for the extension approach to
the training of ministers, as well as the concrete,
practical details of establishing and operating
such a program. A Spanish translation of the third
section of *THEOLOGICAL EDUCATION BY EXTENSION*.
   1969: 256 pp, $3.45. ISBN 0-87808-801-6

ABOUT THE WILLIAM CAREY LIBRARY

William Carey is widely considered the "Father of Modern Missions" partly because many people think he was the first Protestant missionary. Even though there was a trickle of others before him, he deserves very special honor for many valiant accomplishments in his heroic career, but most particularly because of three things he did before he ever left England, things no one else in history before him had combined together:

    1) he had an authentic,personal, evangelical passion to serve God and acknowledged this as obligating him to fulfill God's interests in the redemption of all men on the face of the earth.

    2) he actually proposed a structure for the accomplishment of that aim - he did indeed, more than anyone else, set off the movement among Protestants for the creation of "voluntary societies" for foreign missions, and

    3) he added to all of this a strategic literary and research achievement: shaky those statistics may have been, but he put together the very best possible estimate of the number of unreached peoples in every part of the globe, and summarized previous, relatively ineffective attempts to reach them. His burning conclusion was that existing efforts were not proportional to the opportunities and the scope of Christian obligation in Mission.

Today, a little over 150 years later, the situation is not wholly different. In the past five years, for example, experienced missionaries from all corners of the earth (53 countries) have brought to the Fuller School of World Mission and Institute of Church Growth well over 800 years of missionary experience. Twenty-six scholarly books have resulted from the research of faculty and students. The best statistics available have at times been shaky -though far superior to Carey's - but vision has been clear and the mandate is as urgent as ever. The printing press is still the right arm of Christians active in the Christian world mission.

The William Carey Library is a new publishing house dedicated to books related to this mission. There are many publishers, both secular and religious, that occasionally publish books of this kind. We believe there is no other devoted exclusively to the production and distribution of books for career missionaries and their home churches.

Miss Hilkka Mäläskä, of Finnish nationality, was born in Helsinki, Finland. Under the ministry of the Salvation Army she became converted. Shortly after this she was called to full-time Christian service.

She attended the Lutheran Bible School in Helsinki and the Scandinavian Methodist Seminary in Gothenberg, Sweden, also the European Nazarene Bible College in Schaffhausen, Switzerland. She received her A.B. degree in Religion from Northwest Nazarene College in Nampa, Idaho; her M.A. degree in Theology from Olivet Nazarene College in Kankakee, Illinois. From the Fuller School of World Mission she received an M.A. in Missions.

Miss Mäläskä is a minister in the Church of the Nazarene and has been in much demand as a speaker for churches, missionary groups, and professional organizations, in teaching Bible, Missions, and Evangelism at Olivet Nazarene College in Illinois.